CREATIVE ART
for the
DEVELOPING CHILD

A TEACHER'S HANDBOOK FOR EARLY CHILDHOOD EDUCATION

CLARE CHERRY

DIRECTOR
*Congregation Emanu El Experimental Nursery School and Kindergarten
San Bernardino, California*

P.S

Photography by Samuel A. Cherry

Lear Siegler, Inc. / Fearon Publishers

Belmont, California

To Lynne-Tanya and Neeli

Photo on page 165 by Pat Roper.

ISBN-0-8224-1630-1

Library of Congress Catalog Card Number: 72-81202

Printed in the United States of America.

PREFACE

This book deals directly with ways in which creative art becomes developmental art and, as such, part of the entire growth process of the child—and of the creative growth of you, the teacher, as well. The program described in this book is based on trust, honesty, and acceptance. It is self-starting, self-pacing, and goal directed toward academic and personal achievement. My approach is a personal one, based on more than twenty-five years of experience with children's art.

The child I refer to in this book is between two and six years of age. As the child grows, he becomes able to make certain physical movements at sequential stages of his development. These movements relate to his sensory awareness and his capacity to perceive, which are avenues to cognition. There is, then, to a certain degree, a predictable sequence in the development of perception and cognition in the child, although the precise age at which any specific development takes place varies from child to child. The activities in this book take account of this developmental sequence.

With few exceptions, every activity in this book can be pursued by a four-year-old on his own terms without adult assistance. Many of the activities suggested on these pages are somewhat complex for the two-year-old and should be simplified when they are used with this age group. Many three-year-olds, however, can do the same work as a four-year-old, and some five-year-olds have advanced no further in some areas than the level achieved by some four-year-olds. Occasional reference is made to the older child, meaning a child who is in kindergarten or the first grade. Actually, there is no upper age limit for the use of the material presented in this book. Because the program relies primarily on the choice of materials and the way in which they are presented, a child of *any* age may pursue the activities in accordance with his own abilities and at his own level of creative growth.

The key to meeting the child's needs is your ability to question, listen, and respond—respond to his answers, movements, feelings, and moods. It lies in being sensitive to his behavior when it reflects restlessness or exuberance, loneliness or withdrawal, and to his feelings of hurt, joy, impatience, and wonder. It requires being sensitive to all of the feelings and needs the child brings to school with him —and recognizing your own feelings and needs as well. It is the aim of this book to encourage teachers—and parents—to use this key, not only in meeting the needs of the developing child, but also in helping to unlock their own creative potential.

Throughout the book I have listed the probable growth that will occur as a result of the child's participation in each particular activity. These lists should by no means be considered as separate entities. Each activity is interrelated with many other activities. Learning that takes place in the creative art program is the cumulative result of many experiences and many repetitions of these experiences.

This book could not have become a reality without the contributions, both knowing and unknowing, of so many persons. My greatest debt is to the children I have had the joy of working with throughout the years. They have taught me whatever I know today about creative art for the developing child. Also, it is a privilege to have this opportunity to express my deepest appreciation and thanks to Congregation Emanu El for allowing me the freedom for research and for the support given to the exploratory program that has been developed in the school sponsored by the Congregation. I am grateful to the classroom teachers with whom I have worked—Aileen Applebaum, Lael Cohen, Barbie Gaines, Bettye Kovitz, Mary McDermott, Janet Peters, Alyce Smothers, Barbara Stangle, Halliette Stubbs, and Helen Wallick—all of whom tried out, added to, and encouraged my constant search for methods of presenting and evaluating developmental art. I also wish to thank Dr. Martha Frank for first alerting me to the young child as a medium for creative pursuit; Dr. Donald Churchill, Betty Fauth, Barbara Harkness, Dr. Nikolai Khokhlov, and Betty Zelman for their professional advice; Don Emkens for his darkroom work; Rabbis Norman F. Feldheym and Hillel Cohn for their wise counsel; and the many participating parents who lent their varied talents in so many ways. I also want to thank my husband, not only for his fine photographs, which illustrate this book, but for the frequent exchanges of ideas that made each difficult task seem suddenly easier.

Clare Cherry

CONTENTS

THE CREATIVE ART PROGRAM

Bobby was in his first week of nursery school. Each day when he came home his mother asked, "What did you do today?" His usual answer was, "Oh, nothing. I just played." Then one day he brought home a painting he had made.

He had enjoyed dipping the long-handled brush into the can of creamy red paint. He had enjoyed smearing it back and forth and back and forth over the sheet of paper his teacher had given him. He discovered that if he pressed very hard and rubbed the brush in one little area, he could rub a hole right through the paper. He didn't understand why the teacher gave him the paper to take home. He had already made the hole. Besides, the paint was dry. Dry paint wasn't fun.

But Bobby's mother was excited when she saw it. So was his father. And even the lady who lived next door. But, oh, especially his mother. She told the teacher glowingly how much everyone liked Bobby's picture. Sensing that she had pleased Bobby's mother, the teacher had the child paint another picture the very next day. She soon began to give him more and more art projects to do and they became more and more complicated. Sometimes the teacher had to do much of the work herself, with only a little help from Bobby. Bobby's mother told everyone about the wonderful teacher Bobby had and about the wonderful school he attended and about the wonderful things he made there.

The teacher was really very capable and understanding, but she literally got carried away with her attempt to please Bobby's mother. Bobby's mother was also a very capable and understanding person—but Bobby was always restless and he had been slow in his early growth. His mother had worried about his ability to do well in school. She was delighted and impressed when she saw the wonderful art projects he was bringing home, even though she really knew he couldn't do them by himself.

And so, somewhere between the interweaving of adult dreams and adult anxieties, a little boy's needs were being forgotten.

And what about the little boy? Was he learning anything through doing one complicated art project after another? Well, he was learning how to please adults. He learned that blue at the top of the picture means sky. Circles have to contain eyes, noses, and mouths. When the teacher cuts out something for you to paste, you do it exactly the way she shows you to—after all, she knows what she wants you to make. He learned not to let the paint drip. And he learned that above all—oh, above all—he mustn't ever rub a real hole in the paper.

Each time the child enters the classroom, he will find many activity areas where he can go and start exploring. These areas will be different from day to day and week to week according to the weather, season, number of students, development of curriculum, acquisition of new equipment and supplies, the mood of the children, and the teacher's mood as well. The child will find blocks. Science materials. Puzzles and manipulative games. Things to take apart, connect, stack, fit, sort, arrange, count, divide, balance. Dolls to bathe. Hats to wear. Places to be with others. Places to be alone. Musical instruments. Suitcases to pack and carry. Special things for special days. And *each* day is a special day.

Not only will the materials and equipment be changed from time to time, but the places where the child finds certain things will also be changed occasionally. This kind of variety encourages the child to develop new and challenging ideas and ways of doing things. But enough things will always remain the same to ensure the child's security and comfort of knowing, understanding, and belonging.

Small groups form. If a child finds there is no room for him at one particular activity center, he eagerly approaches another area, because the room is full of challenging things, rich with potentialities for many kinds of learnings.

Conversations spring up among the children and between the children and the adults. Sometimes, however, one child, or two, or an entire group may become so deeply engrossed in creative thought that there is very little talking.

Here and there among the activity centers the child will find art materials. A table with collage materials is on one side of the room. Crayons and paper are on another table. Out of the mainstream of traffic, but obvious, open, and inviting, are areas for painting and for clay manipulation.

The teacher is busy in many parts of the room. She helps one child along a walking board. Another needs his shoes tied. She shares the laughter of two children as they watch a too-high tower of interlocking cubes come tumbling down. Perhaps she discusses with them why it tumbled. She stops to put names on the papers of the children working at the collage table. She helps a child using crayons to spell his own name. And she keeps a watchful eye on the painters and the clay manipulators, assisting them if they need assistance, commenting on the way they are handling the materials, helping them to be fair in taking turns, and generally sharing their feelings as they work. Comments such as, "That bright yellow looks even brighter next to the purple, doesn't it?" or "I see you made a wavy design," are appropriate. Her comments about the actual art work are factual, not evaluative. It is perfectly acceptable, however, to express a positive evaluation of the child's *behavior*. The teacher might say, "I like the way you always put the brush back in the same can it came from," or "I like the way you are sharing the clay," or even, "I'm glad you've learned to share the clay." There are important reasons to talk to a child as he works: Factual comments about his work help him to form concepts and to relate what he is doing to other areas of the curriculum, and evaluative comments about his behavior help him to grow in self-awareness. When such comments are positive, they elevate the child's self-esteem.

A sense of happy and meaningful play, movement, accomplishment pervades the atmosphere. The teacher had come early enough to arrange the room and prepare needed materials before the class session began. Therefore, she is able to fully enjoy, with the children, the free flow of activity from one area to another. It is a beautiful and touching ballet of forms, colors, people, and rhythm.

Art education is a meaningful force in this total learning program. By sensitive planning, the child is motivated to pursue art activities and enjoy experiences that lead to general overall development. He is given plenty of time to move from one step of growth to another at his own pace and in accordance with his own abilities and interests, thus helping him develop strong feelings of self-esteem and self-confidence. As he grows to recognize his own individuality, he becomes better equipped to withstand the emotional pressures of overly structured situations that he will encounter throughout life. By being given many opportunities to become deeply involved in experiences related to touch, smell, vision, and hearing, his sensory-motor development is facilitated. Continued opportunities lead to increased perceptual growth and subsequently to greater cognition. As you acquire an understanding of the developmental process of growth of the young child, you will more fully appreciate your own role in the classroom.

The Developmental Growth of the Young Child

Research indicates that there is a predictable *sequence* in the development of child art. Many factors enter into these predictions, and many contradictory opinions have developed. Relating this sequence, however, to the way the child develops physically makes it easy to understand.

The child develops physically from the top *down,* and from the base of the neck *out* (to his shoulders, arms, hands, and fingers). If the year-old child has a pencil put into his hand, he will usually make vertical scribbles that go up and down if the drawing surface is held up vertically in front of him. If it is flat on a table, his scribbles will probably be horizontal, going back and forth. Either way, they result from the fact that he can only control the movement of his shoulder to make a pumping motion. He has little ability to direct the individual parts of the arm and the hand. His scribbles are the direct result of the physical makeup of his body and the way he is able to make it move.

Gradually, as the child continues to develop, he becomes able to control the movement of his elbow. At this time the lines he draws begin to show slight curves. They begin to run in horizontal or diagonal directions. Although his earliest scribbles were mere accidents of movement while holding pencil or crayon, he now begins to recognize that it is *his* movements that cause the marks to appear on the paper. At this time he experiences the thrill of making something that was not there before. The pleasure derived from this discovery encourages him to develop greater skill. He learns that he can make daubs and scratches and marks, which he often repeats over and over in one area.

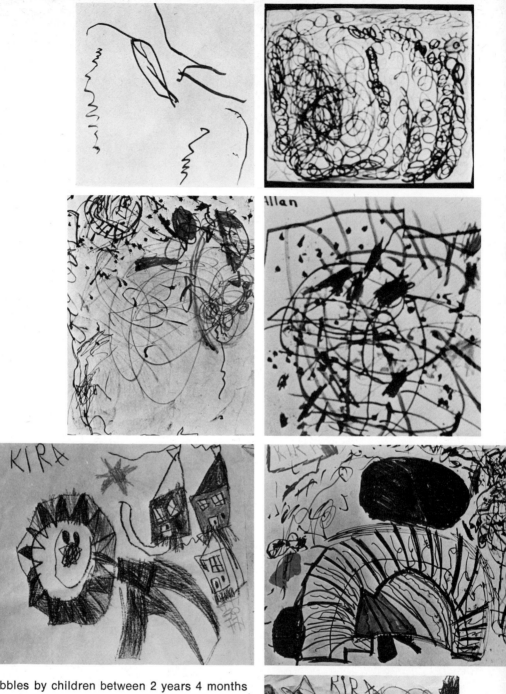

Crayon scribbles by children between 2 years 4 months of age and 5 years 1 month. The child's ability to scribble develops in direct relation to his ability to control his movements and of his awareness of the relationship between himself and the space around him. His marks become progressively more complex as his muscle control develops. The sequence of psychomotor development is approximately the same for each child.

From the elbow, the ability to direct arm movement eventually reaches the child's wrist. He discovers that he can make his wrist move back and forth and round and round. He finds that he can control its movement and, as he practices this new ability, his scribbles become more and more rounded. As this skill increases, he covers his papers with circles, ovals, and spirals.

As the young scribbler continues to practice, he becomes aware of the circles he is able to make. He learns to perceive them as distinct shapes. From birth, the human eye responds favorably to circular or oval shapes similar to the shape of the human head and the nipples on a mother's breasts. The circle is a gentle shape, natural and elemental. From ancient times, it has been used as a symbol of the Self, the psyche. The child's ego and his awareness of himself as an individual begin to surface just about the same time he is developing his ability to draw circular patterns. As his awareness of his ability to control his movement grows, the child begins to try things out, to invent things to do, and to experiment with his ability. When he begins to direct some of the smaller muscles of his hand, his drawings become more complex. Circles become mandalas or radials. This is because he is able to move his fingers in more complicated motions. He makes a circle and, liking what he has made, he decorates it with lines and crosses or other marks. His ability to control his movements and relate to the world outside of himself increases. Then, one day he draws a man.

The notion that a child's first figures are merely oversized heads with legs and arms added is one of the most common misconceptions of children's art. Think of the last time you saw a child draw such a figure. Did he know that hands do not grow out of the ears? Of course he knew. The circle was never meant to be a head in the first place. As far as the child is concerned, the circle *is* the man, the symbol, the complete figure. He may place facial features as a means of identifying his symbol, but it is frequently an adult who first says, "Where are the hands?" Since the child didn't find it necessary to separate the body from the head, he will usually place the hands near the top of the symbol where the shoulders would be if the head and body had been drawn separately. If you ask about legs, the child accommodates you by drawing a pair, even if the symbol was not meant to be a man at all. Perhaps it is a car, or a tree, or even a house. But in the developing imagination of the young child, a car, a tree, or even a house can have legs.

As the child grows, he learns not only to control his arm movements, but the movement of the other parts of his body, too,

Symbolic drawings by children between 3 years of age and 5½. While the child is progressing through the scribbling sequence, he is also beginning to experiment with symbolization, which eventually leads to pure representation. Picture A is a series of circles drawn by a 3-year-old, who apparently recognizes his ability to use them as symbols. As the child develops, he decorates his circles with rays and appendages of all kinds, as we see in B and C, which turn them into suns, flowers, and people. In drawing D, Laura's figure has hands and fingers, legs and toes. She has made the arms different lengths in order to accommodate them to the available space, which is disproportionate as a result of her starting her drawing so far to the left. To balance the figure, she has filled the remaining space with a colorful design. In picture E, Brian identified his circle as an ostrich egg (the teacher wrote the words for him). The two figures with elongated necks may therefore be ostriches. (When the child first discovers how to draw necks, he becomes very conscious of them and exaggerates them in his drawings.) In drawing F, the child has used the circle in all the universal patterns, combining sun, cloud, tree, flower, and person in one design. Drawing G, by a 5½-year-old, shows the child's growing need to communicate. This picture of his environment—including the artist riding a tricycle—tells as complete a story as any written composition.

including his eyes. The normal human eye will take in almost everything that comes into the range of its visual field, but we can *understand* what we see only after we have learned to integrate the sensory input.

Each eye operates independently. Yet the two eyes must be guided to work together. This is done by the brain through a complex network of nerves integrated with the brain cells. These nerves continuously transmit messages that convert what the eye sees into what we perceive. The ability to perceive comes about through the normal process of development.

As the child grows, he learns that things can move toward him and that things can also move away from him. He begins to develop a sequence of skills, each dependent upon those that came before. He learns the concepts of up and down as they relate to his own body and then as they relate to other objects. Later, he learns the concepts of left and right, not by those words at first, but at least in relation to *his* body.

While these skills are being acquired, he learns to coordinate his two eyes to produce an integrated image. This coordination is perfected through his basic movement patterns and explains why eye-hand activities like those required in most art projects are so important to his overall growth.

These eye-hand activities, together with the other natural movements of his body as experienced through play, gradually lead to the understanding of additional concepts such as big and little, wide and narrow, over and under, smallest and tallest, behind and in front of, next to and further away. As the child learns to combine the ability to control his movements with these maturing perceptions, his scribbles, paintings, designs, and arrangements begin to take on pictorial rather than symbolic aspects. His understanding of shapes is now combined with a deeper understanding of three-dimensional forms. As he approaches this level of development, he is still perceiving things from a viewpoint that is different from that of the adult. Because we know how the sequence of his growth and thinking develops, we appreciate this difference. Although we motivate, support, and reinforce his activities, we allow him the satisfaction of making his own discoveries without adult interference.

Evaluating the Child's Progress

To enlarge the scope of your art program, evaluate your materials, the room environment, and your techniques. As your program develops, look for and encourage the child's increasing awareness

A

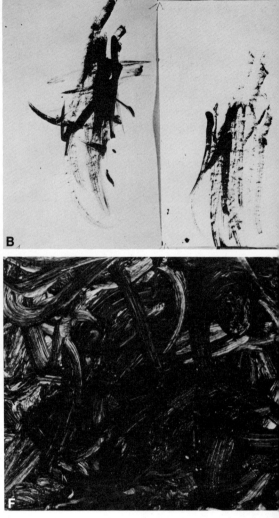

B

TAMMY

E

Seth

I

Ellen

J

Paintings by children between 1 year of age a 5½. The marks in painting A resulted from child's moving his entire arm. In picture B, see two different paintings made on two differe days by a 1½-year-old. Although his marks more deliberate than those of the 1-year-old, t are still the result of whole-arm movement picture C, we can see that the marks made b 2½-year-old are beginning to expand into ov and in picture D they take full circular form picture E, circular masses have given way linear experiments, and mandalas have begu take shape. Picture F shows the next stage development, the child's growing urge to co the entire sheet of paper. He will spend m weeks exploring ways of doing this. Eventu out of the solid mass of paint, new forms be to take shape. In picture G, mandalas and o

10

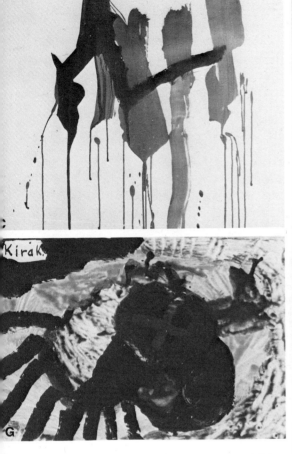

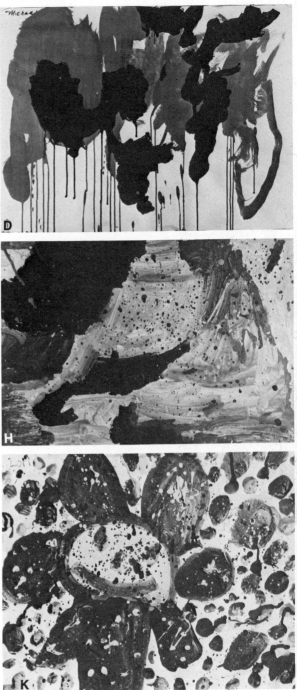

pes of circular shapes reappear as the child
xplores new linear strokes. In picture H, we can
ee that the child has done considerable plan-
ing to produce an intricate design. This careful
lanning shows even further development in pic-
ure I, which is a harmonious blending of various
hades of brown, yellow, and orange. Picture J
eveals even greater development on the part of
 child somewhat older than any of the previous
rtists. When the legs of the figure turned out to
e too short to reach the ground, the artist did
ot lengthen them out of proportion to make them
each. Rather, she filled the space around the
egs with an intricate design, which brought the
ntire figure down to ground level. In picture K,
e design painted by a 5½-year-old in eight dif-
erent colors is a joyful expression of self-esteem.

11

of his own growing creativity and skills. By dating his work, you can save representative examples over a period of time to assist you in recognizing and evaluating his progress. In evaluating the child's progress, do so only in accordance with the way the materials were presented to him and *how* he reacted to them.

Avoid the pitfall of trying to read deep psychological meanings into the child's paintings and drawings. Consider instead *all* of the circumstances under which a particular picture was made and take care not to impose your own prejudices on your interpretation. For example, certain colors have traditional meanings in our society. We know that the child has a tremendous reaction to color and that his paintings are influenced by the colors he chooses. However, he is not yet integrated into our culture to the extent that he is motivated by tradition when he chooses a given color. Though he may be somewhat guided by his emotions, he is limited to choosing from those colors which have been put out for him to use. Even so, a common misconception is that the child who frequently uses black is depressed or troubled. He may actually *be* depressed or troubled, but this may show up more in the way he moves about the classroom, his posture, the expression on his face, the way he applies the paint, or the way he divides up his paper than in his choice of color. The fact is, when a 2½-year-old child uses black, he will probably tell you that "it looks good." What he may mean is that it shows up better than other colors and he used it because he likes for himself and his pictures to be noticed.

Watch a three-year-old or a four-year-old when he chooses black in place of other colors. It may be the color that is closest to him at the time. It may be one that he chooses because his teacher—perhaps because of her own fears—seldom offers it, which makes it new and exciting to him. Once he selects the color he may get carried away with the dramatic impact it makes in relation to the other colors he has already used. Later, after he has covered most of his picture with black, he might tell you, "It's night," or "It's a big, black dog." He might even tell you, if you ask, "It's a man watering the lawn and his breakfast is ready." Again, we must remember that a child's perceptions are not the same as those of an adult. In all probability, he really covered the picture with black paint because black paint, especially tempera, is so emphatic and opaque and positive. Using it makes him feel quite important.

What you should be evaluating in the child's work is the progress he makes from one month to the next in his division and arrangement of space, his awareness of shapes, his ability to control the

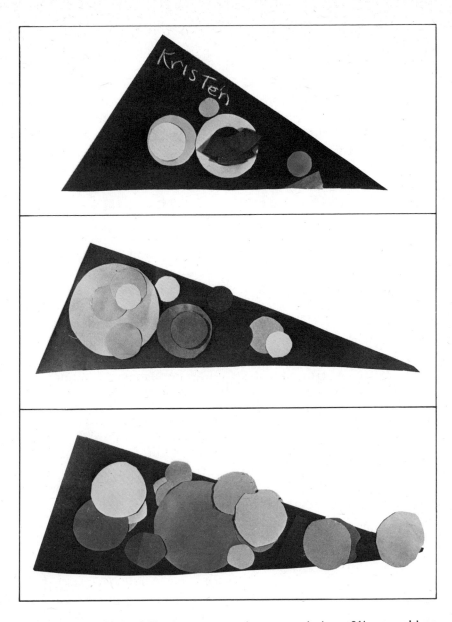

Collage development. The bottom sample was made by a 3½-year-old on her first day at school. She pasted the circles on at random and was not influenced by the shape of the cardboard. The middle piece, made by the same child two days later, shows that she has begun to grasp the concept of seriation in that she started her work with large circles at the large end of the pennant and proceeded to use smaller circles as she moved toward the small end. She also stacked smaller circles on top of larger ones, which she did not do in her first one. In the top sample, Kristen (4) solved the problem of where to place a paper ring that would not fit on the pennant without overlapping by folding it to fit over a circle that she had already pasted on.

movements of his hands and fingers in coordination with his eyes, and his sensitivity to the materials. In looking for these things you will become aware of an emerging sense of color, balance, design, and, above all, creative imagination and inventiveness. You will learn to accept the reality that the creative process is an individual process, that art is a medium that stimulates growth, and that each child must be allowed the privilege of learning through his own experiences.

Implementing the Creative Art Program

The type of material the child uses in the creative art program is not the most important consideration. What he creates with these materials is not the most important aspect either. *The opportunity to use the materials freely is what counts in creative developmental art.* Freedom, however, does not mean that the child is to function without direction. As in all areas of life, things run more smoothly when everyone involved knows what is expected of him. In the creative art program, both adults and children will benefit from the existence of ground rules. A few important guidelines for the teacher are offered in the following paragraphs.

Keeping Hands Off.   Once you have prepared and presented the materials, allow the child to do all the work himself. Let him do it the way he wants to do it. Encourage him to explore, experiment, change, and originate. If you have given him some guidelines for a particular kind of project, let him decide whether to follow them or to ignore them.

Being Involved.   Even though you allow the child to work on a project and use materials in his own way, you should still show that you are interested in what he does. Make him feel comfortable in what he is doing by your sincere show of friendship. He knows that your presence will help him keep his behavior within acceptable limits. Your interest in what the child is doing and your appreciation of what he has made will inspire him when he needs additional motivation or reassurance.

Helping the Child Please Himself.   Help the child understand that he needs only to please himself in what he creates. Help him to know that he is the sole owner of his creations. If you want to keep his work and display it, ask his permission.

Offering Help.   Offer to help the child in learning skills if he indicates his desire and need for such help. Offer help if he loses control of the materials he is using. Also offer to help him in caring for his finished product at the conclusion of the activity.

Avoiding the Use of Models. Adult standards should not be imposed on children's art work. Standards should be derived from the needs and understandings of the individual child. Avoid the use of patterns, coloring books, or mimeographed drawings in your art program.

Interpreting to Parents. Help parents to understand the purpose of creative developmental art. Explain to them the developmental and educational goals. Explain the ground rules. Show the parents by your attitude that you sincerely appreciate each child's efforts. Prepare art displays. Help the parents to understand that the purpose of the child's art work is not just to make something to take home, but rather to meet his developmental needs and to expand the educational program.

Ground Rules for the Child

The ground rules for the child are more specific than those for the adult. Their purpose concerns the safety of the child and the functioning of the class. First, he must understand that tools must be handled with care. He will usually do so if you show him by your attitude that you sincerely trust him to do so. The child must know that he may not use the art materials for touching or hitting children or adults. The child must be aware that the art materials are not to be wasted. They are used only in creating art work. They must not be thrown, deliberately spilled, or destroyed. The child is not to put paste, paint, glue, chalk, and other materials in his mouth. They are not for tasting, eating, or drinking. He must also know that art materials are to be kept in the art area. Each child works on his own project and does not interfere with the work of other children. Painting and other art work is done only on the materials provided for that purpose. Clothing and other children are not to be deliberately painted on. Within these limits the child can be given much greater freedom for self-direction and for self-pacing than if there were no guidelines at all, or if the limits were too many and too restricting.

Your Role in the Classroom

By carefully setting ground rules, you can be free to help the child make the fullest use, according to his needs, of the art materials offered to him. You can help him be sensitive and understanding by being sensitive and understanding yourself. You can help him develop habits of observation, questioning, and listening by your own examples of observation, questioning, and listening. Help him become aware of his feelings and to know that it is all right to express them, sometimes by channeling them into nonverbal means of expression. Help him know that he is free to make choices, and that as long as he demonstrates consideration for people and things he does not always have to conform. Help him know that his independent thoughts and spontaneous actions are appreciated and that imagination is a wonderful thing to have.

The Room Environment

The ground rules will be easier to follow and the developmental goals will be easier to achieve if they are taken into account in planning the room environment. As much thought must be given

One corner of a room for 2½-year-olds. At this age the child needs plenty of room to move around in and many activity areas to explore. No area of the room should detract from any other area. The photograph on the first page of this chapter shows a room for 4- and 5-year-olds.

to the appearance of the room as to its function and use. Even an old building can be enriched by painting the walls in colors that are restful and pleasing to the eye. Worn equipment and furnishings can be made attractive by painting them in light, neutral tones. The addition of brightly colored accessories, which are more readily renewable than the basic equipment, will set off the neutral tones of the older pieces.

To help foster creativity and appreciation of color and design, make use of bulletin boards as an integral part of the creative teaching program. Colors, arrangements, textures, and content should be changed frequently to reflect the time of the year, class activities, special events, and the progress of the class. However, each new display, each picture change, should be handled just as carefully and arranged with as much thought as though the room were being prepared for the opening day of school. Many objects may be displayed around the room. These items should emphasize the effect of color, line, unusual beauty, or some other aesthetic value. There are some simple rules that should be kept in mind in planning the room environment and displaying the children's work.

1. Always remember that the child's eye level is much lower than that of the adult. Displays should therefore be placed low, where the child can approach, touch, feel, and even smell them if he feels like it.
2. A child-oriented room environment leaves plenty of undecorated wall space to allow the child freedom to use his own imagination.
3. When the child's work is displayed, it must not be "improved on" by the teacher for the purpose of impressing other adults. This applies not only to displaying the child's finished work, but also to any of his work that is to be used as part of a larger display. Sometimes a teacher will, for example, cut a child's painting to form leaves, flowers, or other decorative designs. This should not be done unless the child did the work expressly for this purpose.
4. When displays are changed, the teacher should always leave some areas unchanged so the child will not feel uncomfortable in what may appear to him to be new surroundings. Even so, she should change enough things at one time to stimulate and encourage imaginative thinking.
5. From time to time, display reproductions of famous paintings or original art by professional artists. No comments on them are needed except in response to the child's questions.

Arrangement of Furnishings

The room should be arranged in such a way that it can be kept neat and orderly, even though many different activities are going on at the same time. By keeping arrangements flexible, by considering convenience as well as attractiveness, and by helping the child learn to assume responsibility for the appearance of the classroom, the environment can be maintained with ease and order. In a neat and orderly environment, the child's mind is not cluttered and confused by disorder and he is freer to release his own creative thoughts.

Cupboards and Storage Areas

Cupboards and other storage areas should be given as much attention as the appearance of the rest of the room. It need take only a few minutes each day to keep storage areas neat and attractive. Storage containers should be in harmony with the other colors used in the room. One coat of vinyl paint or one strip of decorative contact paper can work wonders with an old cardboard box. Transparent plastic shoe storage boxes, refrigerator containers, colorful baskets, and painted cigar boxes also make attractive storage units. If these storage units have some uniformity of size, it is easier to arrange them neatly. Label everything for ease in finding what you want when it is needed.

The Art Area

The art area may be a permanent place in the classroom, or its location may be changed from time to time. Since the types of activities will vary from day to day, the area that is used should be one that will accommodate the materials and activities that will be involved. Certain aspects of the area, however, should be considered each time.

- It should be away from the general flow of room traffic.
- It should have good lighting.
- It should be close to a source of water, if water is needed.
- It should not interfere with other activities in the room.
- It should be easy to supervise.
- It should have enough room for each child to work in comfort.
- It should not be close to any unprotected surfaces that are hard to clean.
- It should have a place for drying paintings and putting other finished work.

The area used for creative experiences should be so arranged and planned that you will not have to spend your time admonishing everyone to "be careful" or "watch out." If the working surface is not washable, and the medium being used is spillable or splashable, it can be protected by a plastic covering. Use drop cloths, newspapers, or other coverings to protect floors where necessary. Paper or thin plastic can be taped onto adjacent walls to protect them from splattering. A pail of water and plenty of sponges and paper towels should be readily available for emergency cleanups. Broom, mop, dustpan, and other such equipment should be kept nearby.

Child Protection

Protect the child from having to worry about getting his clothes dirty. He will be more comfortable and work more freely if he knows that his school clothes are adequately protected from art materials by an apron, smock, or other coverall. Such items may be commercially purchased, homemade out of plastic, or made from adult blouses or shirts, sleeves cut short and worn backwards. Long sleeves on the child's clothing should be rolled up, and it may be necessary for a child to take off his sweater during an art activity to make him comfortable and give him freedom of movement.

If running water that the child can reach is not readily available, keep one or two plastic buckets of water close by. Add a small quantity of mild soap if you wish. Provide sponges and paper towels. After a preliminary rinsing in the classroom, the child can wash his hands more thoroughly in the lavatory.

Materials

Although materials should not be wasted, they should be plentiful for use by the child as he needs them. Sufficient quantities of materials should be ready before the class begins. It should never be necessary for you to interrupt an activity to prepare additional materials.

Materials should be of good quality. Even when budgets are severely limited, you should not skimp on the quality of paints, paper, and other materials. It is better to offer certain art experiences less often in cases where budget considerations pose a prob-

The art cart. It is mounted on casters so that it can be easily moved from room to room or into the storage closet. The supplies can be changed at any time.

lem. For example, it is not necessary to use paints every day. The painting experience will be far more valuable when the paints are in ample supply and sparkling with color, even if it is limited to one or two times a week. Ways to get the most out of paint materials and to expand the child's opportunities for creative self-expression with less expensive materials, such as newsprint and crayons, are presented in subsequent chapters.

Materials should be attractively laid out. Art supplies should not be kept in torn unpainted cartons. These supplies are *not* waste materials and they should not be treated as such. It is more conducive to the creative use of art media if the materials are in attractive containers. Use painted boxes, colorful trays, plastic carryalls, colored baskets, aluminum or aluminum foil baking dishes, or wooden containers constructed especially for such use.

For liquid media, use either transparent plastic containers or empty frozen juice cans. These cans may be primed with an enamel undercoat and then enameled in various colors—one for each color of paint that is ordinarily used. Several white cans may be prepared for seasonal or unusual colors. Twelve-ounce frozen juice cans make good paint containers because they can support long-handled easel brushes without tipping.

When using such materials as metal lids or egg cartons in various craft projects, have the older children paint them beforehand so that the containers are inviting to use. Do not try to paint plastic containers.

When materials are placed directly on the table they can be set on a contrasting background to keep them visually, if not physically, within comfortable boundaries. Lazy Susans, trays of all kinds, or large sheets of cardboard or paper can be used as boundary keepers.

A small lazy Susan can be enlarged so that it will hold more art materials if you put a circular piece of cardboard or plywood (one that is larger than the existing surface) on top of it. Tri-Wall cardboard, a triple-layered corrugated material, or two or three sections of cardboard cut from corrugated cartons and glued together work well for this purpose. A circular piece of Styrofoam may also be used, but because of its light weight you may have to glue it to the lazy Susan. Sometimes you may divide the lazy Susan tray into pie-shaped sections to separate various types of materials. It is usually more beneficial to the child's development, however, if he is allowed to do his own classifying.

Muffin tins and egg cartons are frequently used as containers to separate collage materials and to hold small amounts of tempera paints (especially for color-mixing experiments). The sturdy white plastic containers that some restaurants receive pastry in are also very useful for keeping materials separated. The transparent plastic pastry containers found in food markets are too flimsy for use in most art projects.

Be on the alert for new types of aluminum or plastic containers in which frozen foods and other products are packaged. You may not be familiar with all of the new packages on the market, but parents are usually very cooperative in letting you know about them and collecting them for your use. Be sure to provide a variety of containers so that the child learns from the start to be flexible in his own choice of materials.

Materials should be readily accessible. Arrange the working area in such a way that the materials can be easily reached by the child who will use them. The materials do not have to be placed right next to the child. Movement is important in all areas of growth. Art is the direct result of certain kinds of movement. For the child to have to move to nearby areas to obtain needed materials and carry them back to his working area is valid for the expansion of needed movement experiences.

Working areas should be varied. When repeating various art activities, change the way you set up the art area from time to time to renew the excitement of exploration and self-discovery. Sometimes you can limit the number of children who may work at a given area to one or two at a time. On other occasions you can set up the art area in such a way that several children can participate at the same time. Table arrangements, materials, and supplies can be varied to add excitement and stimulation to the art program. As often as possible set out only the raw ingredients for the art materials and let the child prepare them for use by himself.

PAPER

Lorraine's grandmother came to visit. She was very much interested in the child's nursery school, and began to question her about it. Four-year-old Lorraine quickly becoming impatient with the cross-examination, said with finality, "Oh, you know. School is where they give you lots of paper to write on."

We take paper so much for granted that we often fail to notice the thrill with which the child reacts to this great motivational material. From neat piles of colored papers on shelves, from large rolls of newsprint or butcher paper in closets, from boxes of scraps and remnants and from piles of old newspapers stacked high—from these come hints of exciting projects and the chance to explore art media, tools, and ideas.

Lack of funds should not keep you from having a good supply of paper because there are many free or inexpensive kinds of paper available. By knowing the characteristics of various types of paper, you can put available funds to good use.

Paper is generally judged by its weight, texture, strength, color, thickness, and opaqueness. The most expensive kinds are made from cloth rags. Most paper we buy today, however, has little rag content or none at all. It is made with wood pulp instead. The greater the wood pulp content, the more quickly the paper will become brittle and yellowed. Because of this factor, even though you may have most of the work at school done on the least expensive papers, occasionally have the child take something home that is on paper of more lasting quality so that his parents can have the thrill of looking at it again in years to come without finding that it has crumbled to pieces.

Many different kinds of paper should be used. The suitability of any particular kind is of little importance to the young child. What is important is the subtle cumulative learning that will come about. The child can become aware of the differences in texture, absorbency, permanency, transparency, sturdiness, and attractiveness of various papers. If the teacher plans ahead of time to change the methods of presenting the projects, to change the shapes, colors, and textures of the paper, each new art activity can be an adventure to the child, and each new type of paper will reinforce what he learned from other types.

General Paper Supply

Manila Paper. This commonly used paper is inexpensive and satisfactory for both painting and drawing. However, it becomes brittle with age, so it should not be stocked too far in advance. If you use it extensively, substitute paper of more lasting quality from time to time.

White Drawing Paper.   Available in many qualities and weights, this is the best all-round type of paper to use if your budget can afford it. The 60 lb. weight is adequate for general use and the 80 lb. weight is excellent. They both take paint well, and are good for cutting, crayoning, pasting, folding, and similar activities.

Mill Screening Paper. Sometimes called oatmeal paper or Roughtex, this paper is good for its textural quality, and is especially good to use with crayons, chalks, and print making. It is available in colors, but is most commonly used in natural or buff.

Construction Paper. This smooth-surfaced, colored paper, is usually obtainable in 80 lb. or 85 lb. weight, and is excellent for general art work.

Poster Paper.   This is similar to construction paper, but is usually of approximately 40 lb. weight. It is easier for the two- or three-year-old to fold and cut than construction paper.

Fadeless Art Paper.   Though light in weight, this paper is durable, strong in color, and suitable for many art activities. It costs slightly more than construction paper, but the fact that it does not fade makes it well worth the difference in cost. It is very easy to fold and cut, and it is especially good for display use. Only one side is colored; the other is white.

Butcher Paper, Wrapping Paper, and Freezer Paper. These kinds of papers can be purchased in rolls through paper supply houses or wholesale grocery outlets. Butcher paper is especially good for fingerpainting, and it can be used for all other types of art activities. Try to obtain it in 30″ or 36″ wide rolls, which will give you much flexibility as to sizes of cut paper. Brown wrapping paper is especially good as background paper for murals and for oversized drawings and paintings. The brown background emphasizes color and design that might otherwise be overwhelmed on stark white paper.

Coated Fingerpaint Paper. Be sure it is of excellent quality before purchasing. Otherwise, substitute other papers.

Oak Tagboard or Index Bristol. Tagboard is inexpensive cardboard, light enough in weight for use in making booklets, greeting cards, folders, and similar items.

Sign-writer's Bond Poster Paper or Banner Paper. This hard, sized bond paper is suitable for oversized paintings, drawings, and murals. Light in weight, it works well for crayon projects. It is 36″ wide and can be obtained in 50-yard rolls at nominal cost.

Free, Salvage, and Remnant Papers

There are many kinds of paper that can be used for art work that do not cost a thing. All that is required is that you locate it and arrange to get it to your classroom.

Newsprint. Many newspaper publishers will gladly give you the end rolls of their newsprint, large stacks of unfolded sheets, or other remnants. Some plants may charge nominal fees for cutting. Newsprint is wonderful for drawing on, and it can be used for oversized floor pictures or murals and for easel painting. It tears easily and is quite absorbent, but for limited budgets it insures having an adequate supply of paper on hand. Colored newsprint is also available. Even though it is not free, it is very inexpensive and will fit into most budgets.

Newspapers. Old newspapers can be used for drawing and painting projects. The printed background, in fact, provides an interesting contrast to paint or crayon. Classified ads and sections without illustrations are the most satisfactory.

Wallpaper. Remnants and samples of wallpaper are sometimes available free of charge from paint stores and decorating shops. Many furniture stores and department stores also give them away. Don't overlook remnants and end rolls that you may have to pay a small sum for. Wallpaper is especially good for painting projects because it is made to take moisture. If the pattern is confusing to the child, let him use the reverse side.

Print Shop End Rolls. Many printers will give you the ends of rolls of paper used for printing as well as scraps of cut paper.

Magazines and Catalogs. Magazines and catalogs can be used for cutting and coloring projects, and the illustrations can serve many educational purposes involving categorizing, comparing, selecting, and other such experiences.

Wrapping Paper. Be sure to save wrapping paper of all kinds. Brown paper bags make excellent paper for art projects. Open wrapped packages by cutting rather than tearing. Cut and trim the paper to usable sizes *before* storing it away. Ask the children's parents to help collect it. For no money at all you can accumulate a large supply of exciting papers for all kinds of art work.

Boxes. Cardboard boxes also make good material for art work. They may be used intact or cut into flat pieces of suitable sizes. Accumulate stacks of all kinds of cardboard that can be painted, pasted, crayoned, and used in many other exciting ways.

Shopping Bags. Save big grocery shopping bags. Cut and opened flat, they are especially good for painting on.

Carpet Covers. Obtain brown wrapping paper that carpets come rolled in. Use for murals, for drawing or painting on the floor, and for other activities inspired by the unusual size.

Other Sources of Free Paper. Check with X-ray laboratories and photographers for the packages in which their films come wrapped. Check with hospitals and doctor's offices, too. Don't overlook the reams of waste paper that you may be able to get from a computer firm or other business that may use large quantities of paper.

Supplementary Paper

You may wish to supplement your basic paper supply with odds and ends of novelty papers such as the following:

Paper plates	Watercolor paper	Gummed crepe
Doilies	Marvalon	paper
Place mats	Fluorescent papers	Tracing paper
Colored tissue	Parchment	Facial tissues
Crepe paper	Japanese rice paper	Corrugated paper
Contact paper	Velour	Cardboard from
Paper towels	Gummed colored	food packages
Sandpaper	paper	Gift wrapping paper

Imagination paper is just what the name suggests. You use *your* imagination to stimulate the child's imagination when he uses the paper. For example, cut sheets of paper in geometrical shapes. Make circles. Make squares. Cut triangular shapes. Cut long, narrow pieces and short, fat pieces. Cut free forms and five-sided or six-sided pieces. Sometimes you can make it into negative-space paper. Cut circles, free-form shapes, and other designs into the paper. Cut large and small holes, balanced and unbalanced designs. Let your imagination be your guide. You can also put marks on it. Mark it with a *B* or an *A* or even a *Z*. Mark it with one dot or two or perhaps three in a row. Make a triangle in one corner and a cross in another. Make two little squares right in the center of the paper. Mark it with pen, paint, or crayon. Mark it big or very small. Mark it fat or mark it narrow. Above all, mark it with imagination.

Use this special paper for any of your creative developmental art projects. Present it with no special comments about its size, shape, or markings. Let the child discover them for himself. Let him cope with the special problems that your imagination may have created for him, and give him the freedom to put his own imagination to work.

Sizes

Just as you vary the shape and kinds of paper, you should vary the size. Although the child requires the opportunity to use his large muscles, and therefore responds well to very large pieces of paper, you should challenge his abilities with many different sizes of paper. Proportions, too, should be varied.

The Scrap Box

If you're like me, you'll have a dozen scrap boxes filled with a priceless collection of odds and ends. We put *all* paper scraps accumulated during cutting activities into our scrap boxes. Whenever anyone uses the scissors, every scrap of paper is saved for future pasting, cutting, and decorating experiences. This year we may be using a box of scraps accumulated two or three years ago. Out of it come the bits and pieces of long-forgotten projects, surprising us with their exciting color, design, texture, or shape.

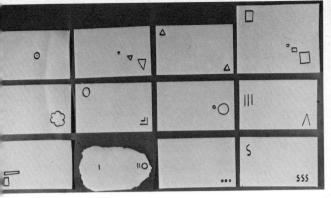

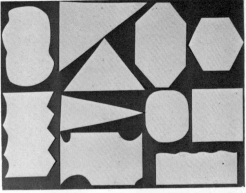

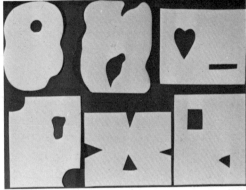

Here are a few pieces of Imagination Paper.

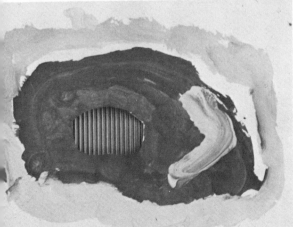

And here are some samples of what 4- and 5-years-olds can do with it.

Give careful consideration to storing your paper. Store it in such a way that you can get to it easily when you need it. Keep different, kinds separated from each other. Always have sufficient quantities readily available for use.

If you don't have large enough shelves for storing large pieces of paper, make portfolios out of the sides of cardboard cartons. Store each type of paper in a separate portfolio. Or use a very large carton as a paper-storage file. To help keep different sizes of paper separated from one another in a limited amount of shelf space, stack the paper flat, storing each size in a flat cardboard gift box. Another way to store large sizes of paper is to make a number of narrow shelves by stacking plywood boards on an existing shelf. Hold the boards apart with blocks of wood, boxes, or bricks.

If you can't find room for very large pieces of paper, simply roll them up. If you have a storage room, leave most of your paper in it, keeping only small quantities of paper on hand in the classroom. This arrangement permits less handling of the paper.

Paper Shapes Through the Year

Concepts can be reinforced and motivation stimulated by varying not only the types and sizes of paper used in art activities, but the shape of the paper as well. The following schedule is one that may be used as a guide and basis for your own ideas throughout the year.

September. Start with circular shapes. The child enjoys round paper for painting, coloring, cutting, and pasting, because it has no difficult corners to cope with. Offer it with crayons and paint. Use round paper for the first cutting experiences. Small paper circles can be pasted on larger circles. Create bulletin board displays with circular-shaped backgrounds. Display round objects in front of them. Also, place round objects in your mystery boxes for feeling and touching experiences. Throughout this month the child should be encouraged to explore, use, observe, and experience round and circular shapes and forms. Allow him to discover the concept of roundness on his own—it doesn't have to be explained. Yet, one day, when you ask the children to sit in a circle, each child will know exactly what you mean.

October.   Introduce rectangular shapes. Ask the child, preferably in small groups of three or four, "What is different about this paper?" Help him to discover that rectangular shapes have *corners*. Reinforce this discovery by finding the corners of objects and by walking to the corners of the room. As the end of the month approaches, return to circular shapes. Present the appropriate colors of paint and watch the child turn these shapes into pumpkins and other Halloween designs.

November.   Pasting, painting, and coloring activities take on a new dimension with the introduction of pennant-shaped paper. Since the child will usually make use of the wide end of the paper first, placing it at his left will encourage a left-to-right progression of arm movements. The use of pennant shapes of paper provides vital learning experiences in seriation. Help the child to discover that pennants have *points*. Pennant shapes can be varied to form leaf shapes, perhaps with many points. Provide the appropriate colors of paint and crayons and the child will produce beautiful fall-oriented designs. Return to round shapes again by drawing circles on bright colors of construction paper for cutting. The resultant "fruit" shapes can be used for Thanksgiving decorations.

December.   Provide the appropriate colors of paint or crayons together with triangular-shaped paper. Then watch the child create beautiful Christmas tree designs. Triangular shapes may also be offered with scissors and paste.

January.   Introduce square-shaped paper. Squares are easy—no surprises, no narrow corners. A square is the same length on each side. A square fits into a circle. A circle fits into a square. A square can be folded diagonally to form two equal triangles. Joining two squares makes one long rectangle. Square paper provides an interesting change from the rectangular-shaped paper used for most art activities. Decorate the room with snowflakes made by having the child help you make cone shapes from square pieces of thin paper and then cutting designs into them.

February.   Folding activities can be continued by folding squares or rectangles over once for cutting heart-shaped designs. The child may decorate these with paint, crayons, or collage materials.

March.   Introduce diamond-shaped paper in time for the kite flying season. (This shape may be used again in May for the Japanese kite holiday.) Diamond shapes are difficult for the young child to comprehend. Try comparing them to squares standing on end.

April.   Oval-shaped paper, decorated with strips of pre-cut ribbons and other trimmings may be used to make beautiful giant Easter eggs.

May.   Scalloped circular shapes of paper may motivate the child to make flower designs, which can be used for Mother's Day decorations and gifts. This shape also works well for Cinco de Mayo designs.

June.   The experienced child will enjoy working with others in making murals on long sheets of wrapping or butcher paper spread out on the floor. These can be decorated with paints, crayons, chalks, or collage materials, or a combination of all.

July.   If it is a hot day, let the child draw or paint on oversized sheets of paper in a variety of shapes on the floor where it is cooler. Provide the appropriate colors of paint and large, rectangular-shaped pieces of paper for patriotic paintings.

August.   Have the child lie down on a large sheet of paper so that you can trace the outline of his shape with pencil or crayon. Let the child paint it as he views himself. The older child may wish to cut it out. After one year of creative art experiences, the painting he produces will probably show a positive self-image.

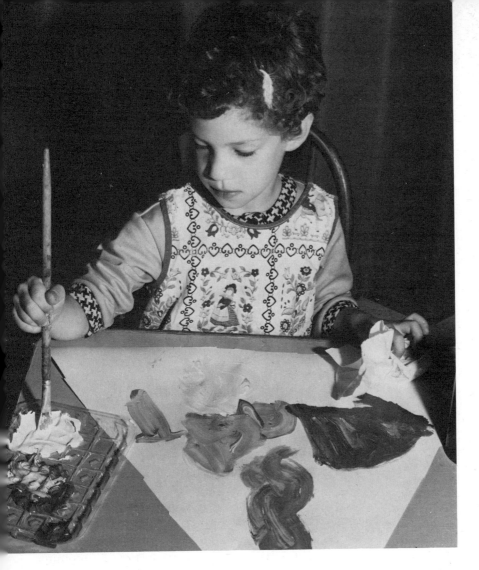

CHAPTER

COLOR

Color is magic. Color is the blue wooly sweater and the green-like-grass top. Color is melting butter on warm toast or sparkling gelatin on crispy lettuce. It's the lipstick Mama is wearing and it's Daddy's shiny brown shoes. It's the flower in the vase and the bicycle on the sidewalk. It's a kitten, soft and furry, and it is also a fish, glistening in the aquarium. Color is the rosy glow of the setting sun and the velvet sky as its shadows deepen with the darkening hour. Color is magic, readily available to all and free for use by the young child. Experience it with him. Take him by the hand and plunge headlong into the very essence of its feelings and its effects. You can afford to be generous. Dish it out in liberal portions and let him know that it thrills you. Share with him its sparkle and its gloss, its quietness and its music, its smell and its touch. And watch him grow.

Color is the *cue* by which we determine the quality of a shape. Although the shape may take precedence in defining what a thing is, it is color that touches more deeply our innermost feelings. The young child between three and five years of age, with normal perceptual development, is more concerned with the colors of objects than with their shapes. Before the age of three, the child is dependent upon tactile cues. He is motivated by whether or not he can grasp a thing, not by what its color is. He needs to touch it with his *entire* hand to find out how it feels, how it is shaped, and what it does. As he becomes more socially oriented, however, and more aware of his own *self* and his own feelings and moods, he is more open to the impressionable effect of color.

Although shape and form are absolute, color is not. A ball is round in any light, though it may appear to be distorted by certain light effects. A square block in the toy box is square on each of its six sides, whether it is barely visible in dim light or strongly evident in bright sunshine. Color, on the other hand, does not remain constant. The slightest change in light will affect it. It varies according to the amount, intensity, and type of light under which it is perceived. A color looks different in the morning sun than in the soft light of a foggy day. It looks different under a Fluorescent lamp than under the light of an incandescent bulb. Each individual interprets the wavelengths that produce color in his own unique way. It is not our need here to understand how light waves are interpreted by the human brain as color, but some simple experiments can pave the way for deeper appreciations of the excitement and vitality of this magic called color.

Color Principles

A goal-directed program of color awareness and self-discovery will help the young child become more aware of his own natural instinct for color harmony. In order to set the stage for such a program, you should have a working knowledge of some of the basic terminology of color and color harmony. Some definitions you should know are listed below.

Hue. A color in its purest form. The term also applies to black, white, gray, and brown.

Primary Colors. Red, blue, and yellow are the primary colors and form the basis for the color wheel. All other colors are a result of some mixture of these colors.

Secondary Colors. Orange, green, and violet are the secondary colors. They are made by mixing equal parts of any two of the three primary colors. A simple color wheel can be made by using the three primary and three secondary colors. All other colors on the color wheel are variations of these.

Complementary Colors. Colors that are opposite each other on the color wheel are complementary. Two colors that are complementary will make brown when mixed. Therefore, brown goes well with any complementary pair. Only one pair of complementary colors should be used at a time. Two pairs will cancel each other out.

Split-complementary. When one color of a complementary pair on a color wheel is replaced by the two colors on each side of it, the three colors then make up a split-complementary. Split-complementaries are easier to harmonize with one another than pure complements.

Warm and Cold.   In general, the colors from yellow through the reds are considered to be warm. Colors from the greens through the blues and violets are considered to be cold. The warm colors have a tendency to come forward; the cold colors seem to recede. All colors are affected by their tints and shades, since the darker tones seem to recede and the lighter tones seem to be larger and closer.

Intensity.   Pure colors are the most intense. Colors are less intense if they contain black, white, or their complementary color.

Tone or Value.   These terms refer to how dark or how light a color is. To darken or reduce the value of high-intensity colors, such as yellow or orange, add black. To increase the value of low-intensity colors, such as violet or blue, add small amounts of white. Too much white, however, will make the color a tint.

Tints and Shades.   Colors to which white has been added are called tints. Colors to which black or their complements have been added are called shades. The shade of a color can also be varied by adding a small quantity of an analogous color.

Analogous Colors.   Colors that are found next to each other on the color wheel are called analogous. They are also called related colors.

Color Experiments and Experiences

Color Magic

This activity demonstrates how colors change when they are mixed with each other. Provide the child with six clear plastic drinking glasses half full of water. Tell the child to put a few drops of red, blue, and yellow tempera paint in three separate glasses. He can then make orange by pouring a little of the red water and the yellow water into a glass; green, by mixing the blue and yellow water; and purple, by mixing the blue and red. Depending upon the child's interest in the activity, you can give him additional glasses and let him experiment further with mixing various colors. After the child has worked with straight color, give him some white paint so that he can experiment with intensity changes. If you prefer, this activity can be done with food coloring or with watercolor paints. If you use food coloring, try to get the kind used by bakeries. This kind has the widest range of colors and intensities. Plastic eye droppers are good to use for measuring out the food coloring. They are available from surgical supply houses.

Color Paddles

Whether commercially purchased or homemade, color paddles can bring the magic of color directly under the child's visual control. To make your own color paddles, cut the centers out of two 3"-square pieces of cardboard. Cover the hole in one piece with colored cellophane. Attach an ice cream stick or tongue depressor to use as a handle. Put the two pieces of cardboard together and attach them with glue or staples. The cellophane and one end of the handle should be between the two pieces. Your color paddle is now complete. Make separate paddles with red, blue, and yellow cellophane. You may have to use two layers of the cellophane, depending on the brand, to make a strong enough color. Have the child experiment looking through the color paddles one at a time and also through different combinations.

Sunshine Windows

On gloomy, bleak days, when the sun has been hiding for too long, make frames by cutting the middle out of small paper plates. Cover the opening with yellow cellophane, attach handles so the children can hold the plates in front of their eyes, and then face the world with "sunshine." The same idea can be used to make "sunglasses" out of tagboard or paper plates.

Color Wheel

Make an oversized color wheel following the directions on page 42. Have the child locate on the color wheel the colors of objects in the room.

Color Walk

Go for a walk specifically to look for colors. How many different kinds of green can you see? Compare the colors of roofs. Collect samples of bark from trees and compare their colors. Find something red. Find something that matches someone's sweater. What color is the sky? The street? The sidewalk?

Autumn Leaves

Collect as many different colors of autumn leaves as possible and use them for displays and collage projects.

Stained Glass Windows

Visit buildings where there are stained glass windows. Decorate a portion of a window in the classroom with colored cellophane to duplicate the effect of stained glass. For a more realistic appearance, use black plastic tape to outline the cellophane as you fasten the various pieces to the window. You might try covering an entire window with one color or with strips of red, blue, and yellow. Try to use a window that will receive direct sunshine at some time during the class day.

Paint Chips

Get two sets of color chips from the paint store. Paste one set on cardboard. Have the children match the colors with chips from the other set.

Color Games

For an active experience with a group of children, play a game like "Policeman, I've Lost My Child."

> *Teacher:* Policeman, I've lost my little girl.
> *Child:* What was she wearing?
> *Teacher:* She was wearing a green and yellow dress.
> *Child:* Here she is.

The child who was found then becomes the policeman.

Colored Lights

Cover the ends of several flashlights with different colors of cellophane. You may need more than one layer to produce strongly enough colored light. In a darkened room, experiment with the colors of the various lights as they interact with one another. Play music during this activity. Light from the flashlights may also be colored by painting the glass ends with transparent watercolor, colored inks, or felt-tip marking pens. An even better effect can be obtained by coloring the bulbs or by using colored bulbs.

Bring an electric food-warming tray to the classroom. Place it at the front right corner of a low table. Adjust the heat to "medium." Provide a box of peeled kindergarten-sized crayons. The child places a piece of paper on the tray. Then he rubs the crayons over the paper. Provide a thick sponge with which he can hold down the paper with one hand. The crayons will rapidly melt onto the paper, producing smears, blotches, and spots of transparent colored wax. Held up to a window, the paper will have the brilliance of stained glass. Try many different types of paper. Each kind produces a different effect.

Melted Crayons.

Another interesting color experiment requires the use of marbles. Provide several small dishes of paint with several marbles in each one. Place a sheet of paper on the bottom of an open cardboard box. The paper should be the same size as the bottom of the box. Provide teaspoons which the child can use to dip the painted marbles from the dishes. He drops them into the box and rolls the box back and forth and side to side, noting the colored lines formed by the paint coming off the marbles.

Color Guide Through the Year

Use this basic color guide to plan for increasing the child's color awareness. Don't try to do all these things in any one year, but use them as the taking-off point for your own ideas. Refer to this guide when planning what basic colors of tempera to make available, what crayons to use, and what colors of paper to provide. Intersperse these various ideas with general selections of colors. Start using the guide in September.

1. Red, blue, yellow   Primary colors only.
2. Red and blue only.
3. Yellow and blue only.   Mix these colors to make green. Compare with leaves, grass, flower stems. Be sure to do this before all greens fade into autumn colors.

4. Yellow, blue, green.
5. Red and yellow only.   Discuss resultant orange. Compare with the colors of citrus fruits—oranges, lemons, tangerines.

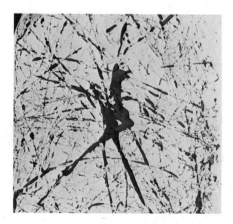

Marble Rolls.

6.	Yellow and orange.	Halloween is approaching.
7.	Orange and black.	Use orange paint on black paper or black on orange.
8.	Orange, black, white.	Vary colors as above.
9.	Yellow orange, orange, red orange, yellow.	Compare with the colors of raw and cooked pumpkin.
10.	Red, orange, yellow, green.	Use on brown paper for an autumn effect.
11.	Brown, yellow, red orange.	Autumn-leaves effect.
12.	Orange, green, violet.	Secondary colors only.
13.	Orange, green, violet, red, blue, yellow	Primary and secondary colors.
14.	Red and green.	Christmas is approaching.
15.	Red, green, blue.	
16.	Magenta and yellow green.	A unique Christmas combination.
17.	Dark green, bright green, dark red, bright red.	Also for Christmas.
18.	Blue and orange.	It's Chanukah time, too.
19.	Turquoise blue and orange.	
20.	Two or three shades of blue plus white.	Also for Chanukah.
21.	Blue, green, magenta, white.	Use on black paper.
22.	Complementary colors.	Use only one pair at a time, with black and white or brown and white.
23.	Analogous colors: Magenta, red, red orange, orange; blue, blue green, green, yellow green; green, yellow green, orange, yellow orange; violet, magenta, blue violet, blue.	Rainy days bring plenty of time to experiment.
24.	White.	Use on black paper on a snowy day.
25.	White and black.	Use on blue paper on a foggy day.
26.	Red, white, blue.	February brings patriotic holidays.

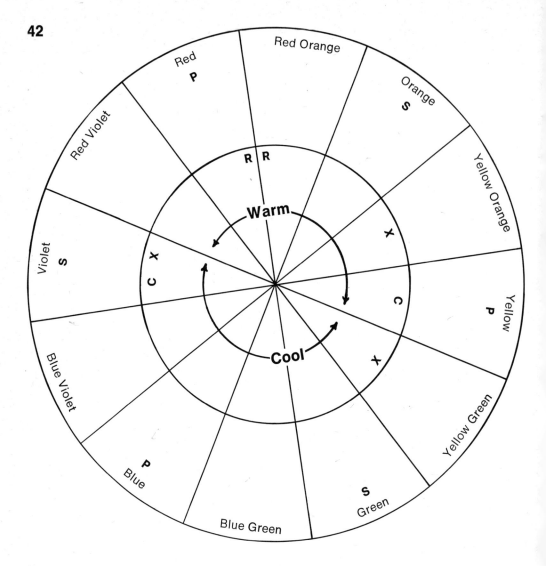

Color wheel. Using transparent watercolors, crayons, or oil pastels, you can make your own color wheel on this form by following these simple directions. Put each primary and secondary color in its own space in the outer ring of the circle *and* in the space on either side of it. The overlapping colors in every other space will form combination colors: red violet, red orange, yellow green, blue green, and blue violet. (Blue violet is very difficult for the young child to distinguish from blue. Do not expect him to be able to.)

Key

P Primary color
S Secondary color
R Related color
C Complimentary pair
X Split complimentary

27. Red, pink, white.	Valentine's Day is coming.
28. Red, pink, white, light blue.	Unusual Valentine colors.
29. Red, magenta, pink, light blue.	
30. White with primary colors.	Add the white to each color experimentally.
31. Black with primary colors.	Add the black to each color experimentally.
32. Black and white with primary colors.	Add the black and the white experimentally.
33. White with secondary colors.	Add the white to each color experimentally.
34. Black with secondary colors.	Add the black to each color experimentally.
35. Several pastel tints of *one* color.	
36. Several shaded pastel tints of *one* color.	Made by adding minute quantities of black to pastel tints.
37. Six different pastel colors.	Spring is here.
38. Red, white, and green.	Cinco de Mayo. These are the colors of the Mexican flag.
39. All colors, including some tints and shades.	Provide twelve to fifteen different colors from which the child may select his paints.

CHAPTER

4

CRAYONS

The waxy smell of the rub-it-hard-until-it's-shiny crayon! The smoothness of the waxed-over surface! The thrill of getting a brand new box of crayons and trying out each color! The delicate shadings of the rub-it-lightly-like-Mama-does picture! The scribbles and the scribble pictures! And, the exciting sheets of paper where the crayons leave their beautiful marks.

Few art materials are as familiar to the average adult as crayon and paper. Few materials have been used so extensively in all areas of art activity and at all levels of development. And yet, we find that their importance is frequently minimized. They are but lightly considered in many art books. Crayons are wonderful tools for a child's first beginning scribbles. They are easy to manipulate and control. Using crayons leads to learning, growth, and development.

Crayons are important in the development of writing skills. The child can practice moving his arm, wrist, and lower palm rhythmically on a table top or floor, as he pushes a crayon back and forth and round and round. This prepares him for writing where similar, but more controlled, motions are necessary.

Crayons are also important in developing figure-ground discrimination, symbol recognition, and symbol formation. Although the child makes similar movements when he uses a paint brush, the symbols formed with a brush are usually less distinguishable to him than the finer-lined drawings made with a crayon.

Crayons are dependable and readily available. Unlike paints, they don't need water or refilling or adult assistance. A child can get them out of a cupboard or off of a shelf and, without any help from anyone, use them. Although the child may need to be reminded that walls and furniture are not for drawing on—that crayons are to be used only on paper or other specially provided materials—he is able to use them independently, which is an important ego-developer.

Crayons are important because of their beautiful colors and because of the exciting world they help the child to bring within the realm of his own control. Crayons make the sun yellow, the grass green, and flowers blue and purple and red. They can make rosy cheeks and smoking chimneys. They can make rainbows.

Crayons are also important because they can be used to express feelings and satisfy emotions, even in the two-year-old as he thrills to the kinesthetic sensation that his scribbles produce within him.

Crayons, the A-B-C of art, should be presented to the child with excitement and care. They should be stored where the child can get them at will. They should be kept in sturdy, neat containers, rather than in boxes out of which they may need to be shaken. They should be kept in groups of selected colors, rather than all mixed up so that one box contains brown, black, and purple, another has reds and greens, and no one seems to know what happened to the orange and the yellow.

Until the child has reached the age of five or six and has gained

Large kindergarten-size crayons and a long roll of paper provide endless fascination for David (4). Placing the paper on his right encourages him to work from left to right in preparation for future writing experiences.

some control of the fine muscles of his fingers, and especially his fingertips, he should be given crayons that are large enough to be grasped with the whole hand. Kindergarten-size, non-roll crayons are preferable, but any thick, good-quality crayon will do. They should be waxy but hard enough to resist breaking.

A selection of regular-sized crayons of many colors may be made available for occasional experimentation. These crayons will break and the child will tire more easily when he uses them. But he should find this out for himself and have the opportunity to try them out to verify his own progress from time to time. When he is ready for more delicate fine muscle movements, he should be given regular crayons.

You may want to keep a supply of peeled crayons to be rubbed lengthwise over the paper. If some of the crayons are both peeled and notched the child can experiment with special effects.

Keep a separate supply of black crayons to give to the child from time to time for outlining paper collage, especially when he is working with cut-outs of geometric shapes. At the age of two, the child will scribble over his collage with the crayon. As his perceptual powers develop, he will gradually begin making vague outlines around some of the shapes. Eventually he will clearly emphasize the geometric shapes with the black crayon. These are natural processes and the child does not need to be given directions. Simply give him the crayon after he finishes his collage.

From time to time the older child may be given a black crayon to use in outlining colors in his tempera paintings. This will increase his awareness of how he is utilizing space and color.

Sometimes the child should be given his own container of six or eight colors of kindergarten-sized crayons. He should be encouraged to keep the crayons to the left of his paper. Some days he should be asked to share crayons with others. Once in a while the crayons to be shared should be all mixed together in a basket, painted cigar box, plastic bowl, or other container. Selecting crayons from a container placed in the middle of a table calls for a different type of eye-hand movement than the child uses when he has his own box at the side of his paper.

One of the positive qualities of crayons is that they last a long time. Even so, bring out a new supply once in a while to replenish the assortment.

Teach the child that dark-colored crayons are softer than light ones because they contain a greater quantity of wax, which makes them opaque. When the child uses them to color over paper or

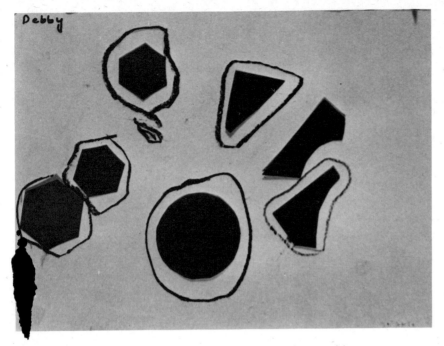

Geometric shapes outlined in black crayon by a 4-year-old.

lighter colors of crayon, the colors underneath won't show through. Lighter-colored crayons are harder because they contain less wax than the dark ones. This hardness keeps them from adhering heavily to the surface they are covering. Because of this hardness and because they contain a smaller quantity of wax, light crayons are more transparent than dark ones. Being transparent, they can be used to produce change according to the colors of paper on which they are used.

Save the stub ends of old crayons to make SCRIBBLE COOKIES with. Simply peel all the paper off of the crayons. Separate them by color and break them into small pieces. Put the pieces of each color in separate sections of a muffin pan. Place the pan in a warm oven with the heat *turned off,* and let the crayons melt slowly. When they are fully melted, remove the pan from the oven and let it cool. You will end up with Scribble Cookies, bright, shiny, and new. The child can grasp them with his entire hand. They are great for rubbing, scribbling, and general experimentation. Since the temptation to bite into one of these enticing cookies is sometimes overwhelming, the very young child needs to be reminded that they are not real cookies and that they are not to be eaten. Commercial kits may also be purchased to use for the renewal of old crayons.

Whether you offer the child inexpensive newsprint or fine white drawing paper reserved for special occasions, almost any kind of paper is satisfactory for use with crayons. Rough-textured papers are especially interesting. Any color of paper can be used, each offering a new challenge and a new experience as the child discovers for himself that certain colors of crayons don't show up well on certain colors of paper, and that others offer a good contrast.

In addition to the ordinary rectangular shape, paper may be round or square or triangular. It may be cut into free forms or into many-sided geometric shapes. It may be torn around the edges. It may be very large, medium sized, or very small. Each new shape, each new size, promotes the cognitive growth of the child.

What To Do with Crayons

The main thing to do with crayons is to *make them available*. They should have a place on the toy shelf along with puzzles, manipulative toys, blocks, games, and other educational materials. Paper, too, should be readily available so that the child may use the crayons during any period when he has a choice of activities.

The child should have many opportunities each week to simply scribble on different shapes, sizes, and types of paper—especially on large sheets of paper on the floor or on a table. Only through the repeated practice of the movements involved can he acquire a *meaningful* control of those movements.

Many crayon techniques can be introduced to the child from time to time as a further means of experimenting with and exploring the medium. A few suggestions follow.

Color Changes

Give the child blue paper and yellow crayons. The child will see that the yellow crayon makes green lines on blue paper.

Variations
- Use red paper with white crayons to make pink.
- Use red paper with yellow crayons to make orange.
- Allow the child to make a free selection of colors of crayons and paper.

Baskets of crayons and plenty of paper are always available in this toy cupboard for the child to use when he wishes.

● Encourage the child to achieve the same types of color changes with different colors of crayons rubbed lightly over one another on white paper. (The sides of peeled crayons are best for this effect.)

Result: These experiments with the possibilities of color changes will give the child an awareness of the versatility of crayons. His knowledge of color relationships and their effect on one another will be increased. He will develop a greater understanding of cause and effect and of the fact that he has the ability to control the materials.

Textured Papers

Provide several different kinds of textured papers, such as sand-paper, small pieces of watercolor paper, and oatmeal paper. Allow the child to make his own selections. Encourage him to draw or scribble on them with crayons.

Variations
- Substitute textiles for papers.
- Use wood to draw on.
- Prepare special drawing paper by having the child first coat a sheet of paper with white tempera paint, or any other light color. The crayon will adhere to the tempera-painted surface with an interesting textural effect.

Result: The child acquires knowledge that will lead to an ability to classify materials according to texture. He also learns to discriminate in his selection of materials.

Crayons and Fingerpainting

Provide fingerpaint paper, butcher paper, or something similar. Provide crayons and fingerpaint. Make a padding of several thicknesses of newspaper to put under the paper. Then have the ch color heavily on the paper. He can then use the crayoned pap for fingerpainting.

Interesting effects can be achieved by controlling the colors given to the child. For example, use only blue and green crayons with red and yellow fingerpaint. Use red, yellow, and orange crayons with blue and green fingerpaint. Use yellow, green, and black crayons with red and blue fingerpaint.

Result: The child's sensitivity to color increases as he becomes interested in experimenting with new color combinations on his own. He becomes more aware of the type of linear designs he makes and more conscious of his ability to control his own movements and to cause changes.

Scratch Boards

This activity is a difficult one to use with children under five years of age because it takes a great deal of preliminary preparation. However, if it is done on a fairly small piece of paper, even the four-year-old child can derive a great sense of accomplishment in what to him seems like magic.

The project requires a piece of paper or cardboard with at least two layers of crayon, one on top of the other, to create a surface into which a design may be scratched. This is sometimes called *sgraffito,* an Italian term meaning to score or scratch and referring to designs scratched into plaster, revealing a different-colored surface underneath. This technique is also referred to as crayon engraving or crayon etching.

Give the child a piece of smooth or slick-surfaced paper or cardboard and different colors of good-quality, waxy crayons. Have him cover the entire surface of the paper, or a marked off section (for example, a 6″ × 6″ area on a 9″ × 12″ sheet of paper), heavily with color. Then put another layer of color over the bottom layer. Solid black works best for the top layer. Rub the top layer with a paper towel, tissue, soft rag, or even the hand to give it a buffed appearance. Then, using a 3-inch nail, a pointed stick, a toothpick, a nail file, or some other pointed object, scrape a design into the surface, revealing the underlying colors.

Variations
- Use black tempera paint instead of crayon for the top layer. The consistency should be thin and creamy.
  Add a small amount of liquid soap to help the paint adhere to the waxy bottom layer.
  Use other colors of tempera for the second layer.
- Dust the bottom layer with chalk from a blackboard eraser to increase the adhering power of the tempera. Use diluted India ink for the top layer.
- Use dark-colored crayons for the bottom layer and paint over it with white tempera to achieve a completely different effect.

Result: The child's consciousness of cause and effect increases. His knowledge of linear design and color contrasts is strengthened. This extended project increases his powers of concentration.

Arm Dancing

Arm Dancing is an excellent developmental exercise. It is especially helpful for a child with visual or auditory perceptual difficulties. Place a very large sheet of paper on the floor. Set out crayons at intervals along the length of the paper. Prepare a series of short musical selections to play on a record player. They may be folk songs, dance music, children's songs, or classical pieces. Have each child get down on the floor on his knees and tell him that he can use a crayon to do "arm dancing" on the paper. Five or six chidren can work along each side of a 36″ wide sheet. When the music is turned on, the child begins to draw. (He may need to be reminded at the beginning to make his entire arm "dance" and not just his hands.) After a few minutes, stop the record momentarily and change to a different selection. Have the child use a different crayon each time the music is changed.

Arm Dancing, a group activity done to music. These children are all 3 years old. People of all ages perform this activity exactly the same way.

Variations

- Use two arms to "dance" with.
- Place paper cut-out shapes underneath the drawing paper. Shapes will take form as colors are drawn over them.
- Have the children do arm dancing while standing at a table instead of kneeling on the floor.

Result: The child increases his ability to control the use of his muscles to scribble smoothly and rhythmically. He develops his visual-auditory perceptual powers and increases his overall sensory awareness. He releases pent-up feelings and eases his tensions. When using both arms, he develops the bilateral coordination of the body. When paper cut-outs are employed, the child's awareness of shapes is increased and he begins to develop an understanding of the constancy of given shapes.

Representational Drawings

The nursery school child should not be made to feel that he *must* make a representational drawing at any time, nor should he be "taught" how to draw certain objects or figures. However, as he begins to show intense interest in representation, which may occur around age five or five-and-a-half, occasional suggestions may be given him. If suggestions are in order, encourage the child in an appropriate way. For example, you might say, "If you like, you may draw a picture of yourself," or, "Now that we've talked about animals in the zoo, you may draw a picture of an animal." Another imaginative approach is to say, "If you were an animal, draw a picture of how you would look."

Result: The child increases his awareness of his ability to control his own movements. He has the experience of making a plan and completing it. He develops his ability to transfer visual information and memories onto paper, which is an important part of his cognitive growth.

Crayon Rubbings

From infancy we depend greatly on our sense of touch to tell us minute details that our eyes fail to reveal about certain objects. And yet, from an early age children are told to keep their hands off of things. The nursery school teacher has the opportunity to *encourage* touching. She should stimulate it, talk about it, and, above all, learn to be creative with it. A good way to stimulate and develop the child's sense of touch is to make rubbings.

The simplest kinds of rubbings are made with peeled crayons on typing paper. They should be started with a somewhat structured technique, in which you place some textured material under the paper for the child. When he rubs the side of his crayon lightly over the paper, the shape or design will appear on the paper. Start with paper doilies or with simple geometric shapes cut out of construction paper. Then encourage the child to make his own arrangement of things to use in creating a design on paper.

Result: The child learns about textures. He increases his awareness of cause and effect, and he learns that something doesn't have to be visible to the eye to cause a change. He also becomes aware of delicate shadings he can make with crayon.

Nature Rubbings

Make crayon rubbings by placing paper over leaves and other growing things. Ferns can be used to make especially beautiful rubbings. Try different kinds of tree bark, both the outer side and the underside. Encourage the child to use grass, clover, and any other things that strike his fancy. Give him the freedom to experiment with the ridiculous if he wants to. Let him make his own discoveries. This is the nature of creative art for the developing child.

Result: The child's awareness of the differences between shapes and textures is strengthened, while at the same time he develops consciousness of the constancy of certain shapes and textures. He increases his ability to make tactile discriminations. He develops an understanding of *over* and *under* and of *thickness* as opposed to *flatness*.

String, Yarn, and Other Wiggly Things

Experiment with string, yarn, ribbon, rubber bands, thin wires, pipe cleaners, and other wiggly or flexible things that the child can manipulate with his hands and fingers to form the design for his rubbing. This shaping and forming requires fingertip touching and enables the child to explore the textural surface of the material. As he arranges the design and bends and shapes tiny wires, he uses the small muscles of his fingers. Each new muscular movement is an important part of the child's development. Children may pair off to assist each other in holding the paper firmly.

Crayon Rubbings made by rubbing the sides of crayons over objects with interesting textures.

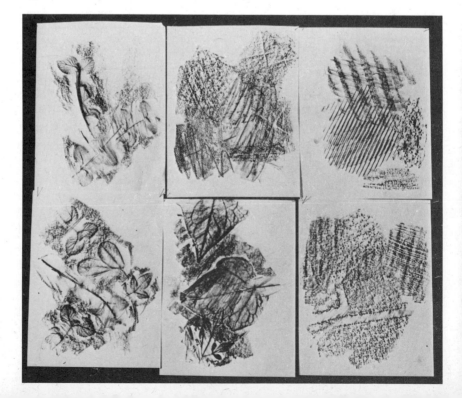

Crayon Resist. Jenny and Matt (both 4½) are covering their papers with crayon. Then they will cover them with a thin wash of black tempera, which will enhance the brilliance of the colors. Scott (5) has already finished his.

Result: This activity increases the child's awareness of the possibilities of linear designs and shapes. It strengthens his manual coordination in two important ways: The child exercises the use of the small muscles in his fingers and hand, and practices the control of muscular pressure as he tries to keep from tearing the paper while rubbing over it.

Rubbings Walk

Another intriguing activity is a Rubbings Walk. With crayon and paper, march around the room. Explore every nook. Try out every kind of surface. Look into drawers. Let the child find tempting surfaces to use for rubbings. He'll make many mistakes. Some things will make the paper tear, but that is something he should find out for himself. He may find that he can use a flat metal washer to make a donut-shaped design, but thicker rubber washers won't work. But one thing he will find out, and that is how to make rubbing designs of things you have never thought of.

Result: The child practices making choices and decisions. He learns to discriminate among alternatives and he grows in his understanding of the physical world.

Use good white drawing paper, butcher paper, tagboard, or any other paper with a smooth, but not slick, surface. Provide crayons and either thinned tempera paint, watercolor paints, or colored inks. Make a padding of several thicknesses of newspaper to put under the drawing paper. This will provide a cushion to make the crayon marks more intense. The child makes a design on the paper with the crayons. He should be encouraged to press hard in order to give the finished design a heavy, waxy surface. When the drawing is completed, the child paints over the entire paper with the liquid paint, watercolor, or ink. The waxy surface will repel the liquid, which will adhere only to the background areas.

Variations
- Use only light-colored crayons and dark paint. You may want to reverse the procedure and use only dark-colored crayons with light paint.
- Use colored ink for the liquid covering or diluted black India ink.
- Wet the entire sheet of paper with water and allow drops of color to spread over the background.
- After the child has had some experience with this activity, give him a piece of wax or a wax candle to use in drawing a picture on white paper. The wax will not show up until he paints a thin wash of paint or ink over it. (*Note:* If too much of the crayon design has been obliterated by the liquid covering, run water over the design to remove some of the overpainting. This is especially effective when the crayon drawing has been given a very heavy coating of black tempera. When washed off, enough of the black will adhere around the edges of the crayon marks to give the entire picture a batik effect. Care must be taken not to tear the paper in wetting it. A piece of paper can best be handled by placing it on a board or tray before putting it under running water.)

Result: The child observes that a surface covered with wax or wax crayons will repel a liquid substance. He develops his small hand and finger muscles as he exerts pressure on the crayons to obtain more brilliant colors. He increases his awareness of linear patterns and color contrasts. The child usually takes special pride in his completed crayon resist pictures, because of the aesthetic effect of even the simplest design.

5

OTHER DRAWING MATERIALS

Soft, colorful, powdery chalk. Dry, talcumy, comfortable chalk. Like fine, dry dirt you may have played with on a hot summery day. It even clings to your hands like dirt, and if you touch something, the color comes off on what you touch.

Chalk

The tactile effect of chalk, as it so lightly and so easily leaves its marks, is irresistible. Whether it is white chalk on a blackboard, large, colored, lecturer's chalk, or bright-colored oil pastels on a big piece of scribble paper, chalk is irresistible.

Dry Chalk

Provide white or light-colored chalk and dark paper, or use dark chalk with light paper. If you are using colored chalk, provide soapy water, sponges, and paper towels to help the child keep his hands clean. Encourage the child to use the ends and the sides of the chalk.

Variations
- Use highly textured papers, including sandpaper, to achieve unusual effects.
- Make textured rubbings, as with crayons, by placing various textured objects under the paper.
- Squares of Masonite can serve as individual chalkboards on which to draw. The Masonite can be sprayed with blackboard paint if desired.

Result: The child develops awareness of color. He learns that his control of the pressure he exerts on the chalk affects the intensity and density of the color he is using. Chalk requires the application of much less pressure than crayon, and this difference often alters the kinds of linear designs the child produces.

Use chalk on good quality drawing paper that has been dipped in water or moistened with a sponge. Use small sheets so that the paper will not dry out before the drawing is finished. Place wet newspapers or paper towels under the paper to help keep it moist.

Result: The child increases his sensitivity to color as he sees that the chalks become brilliant on contact with the wet paper. He extends his knowledge of materials and becomes aware of new linear patterns.

Buttermilk

To keep the chalk from rubbing off, wet the paper with buttermilk. Large sheets of paper may be used because paper moistened with buttermilk will not dry as rapidly as paper moistened with water.

Variations
- Use liquid starch instead of buttermilk or use canned milk diluted with liquid starch to provide a more permanent finish.

Result: The child increases his knowledge of cause and effect, as he discovers that the colors are not only intensified by the starch or buttermilk, but that they will not rub off when the paper dries.

Fingerpaint

After doing a chalk drawing using the buttermilk or starch method described above, the child decorates his picture with fingerpainting. Only the powdery material on the surface of the chalk will spread around with the liquid, so this project works best with a heavily chalked picture.

Result: The child discovers that *some* of the chalk fuses with the liquid, but not all of it. He learns that chalk is a less constant medium than crayon.

Wet Chalk

Instead of wetting the paper with water, buttermilk, or liquid starch, dip the chalk itself into a liquid. Provide small individual containers or a large one to be shared by several children.

Christine and Scott (both 5) experiment with chalk scribbles on paper covered with liquid starch.

Result: The child develops a better understanding of the relationship between chalk and liquids and discovers that an aim can be achieved in more than one way. He acquires the necessary background to build an understanding of the difficult concept that some steps in a process can be rearranged or reversed, still producing the same result.

Sugar Water

Make a solution of one-third cup of sugar to one cup of water. Soak the chalk in this solution for five or ten minutes before the child uses it. Allow the child to choose his paper from a variety of sizes and textures. The chalk may be kept wet by repeatedly dipping it into the sugar water as it is being used.

Result: The child observes the increased brilliance of the colors, and learns that this is caused by the reflections from the sugar crystals, even though they are not easily visible. He increases his awareness of cause and effect. This activity also contributes to his aesthetic growth. In selecting his own paper the child practices making choices.

Oil pastels are similar to both chalk and crayons. They may be used like either one. They do not rub off as easily as chalk, are not as messy, and are more easily controlled. They are not as hard as crayons, and encourage greater freedom of movement because they require less pressure to obtain brilliant colors. Provide oil pastels and good drawing paper. This medium works best on paper that is not smooth.

Variations
- The older child may blot the finished art work lightly with a cloth that has been dipped into a *small* quantity of paint thinner to create an oil-painting effect.
- The child can achieve a very different effect by combining oil pastels with crayons.

Result: The child reacts to the fluidity with which the oil pastel goes on the paper. He finds that he is able to control the colors by the amount of pressure he exerts.

Felt-Tip Pens and Markers

The transparency, brilliancy, and free flow of the colors of felt-tip pens make them a definite asset to any art program for young children.

Although colors of permanent-color felt-tip pens and markers are more brilliant, watercolor felt-tip pens are more appropriate for the very young child because the paint is washable. Felt-tip pens may be used on almost any surface, including fabrics, wax paper, and plastic. Except for black, the colors do not show up well on dark-colored paper because of their transparency. Interesting effects, however, may be obtained by using lighter colors of paper. Felt markers may be used for almost any activity that calls for pen, pencil, or crayon. Simply provide felt-tip pens and paper, cardboard, or some other material on which they may be used, and let the child use them as he wishes. Protect the surface on which the work is placed, because the color may "bleed" through the paper. Felt-tip pens are fairly expensive and must be taken care of to ensure that they do not dry out too quickly. Therefore, the child *must* learn to put the cap back on each pen after he uses it.

Drawing with felt-tip pens. Varying stages of muscular control are evident in these drawings by Stephanie, Kerry, and Brian (all 3½) and Laura (4).

Variations
- Use felt-tip pens for "arm dancing."
- Use felt-tip pens instead of tempera or watercolor paints to make resist painting.
- Decorate plastic containers with them, or use them on wax paper to create a stained-glass effect.
- Sometimes use them to decorate fabrics.

Result: The child increases his awareness of color differences, linear design, and transparency. He learns to control the muscular pressure he uses in order to take advantage of the "free-flowing" quality of the pens. This control, and the resultant lightness of touch, leads to an increased freedom of arm and hand movement. The child also learns the importance of taking care of materials and, in so doing, develops his sense of responsibility.

Glass Wax

Give the child some glass wax and a cloth. Let him cover an area of window glass or mirror with the glass wax. When the glass wax is dry, the child uses his fingers or hands to make a design on the glass.

Result: The child is surprised by the ease with which he can make clear marks on the window with a very light touch of his fingers. He extends his sensory and kinesthetic awareness. He realizes the finality of his movements in this medium (unlike crayons or paints), for once the wax or mud is removed, he can't change his marks.

Mud or Wet Sand

When you are outdoors with the child, find some mud that is not too wet or some wet sand. Make designs in the mud or sand with sticks, twigs, or other "found" tools.

Result: The child learns that he has the ability to control materials by exerting more or less pressure. He experiences satisfying

A bowl of mud and a little encouragement from the teacher started Kristen, John, and Leo (all 5) on a unique drawing experience which provided much kinesthetic satisfaction. Afterwards, the teacher and children together cleaned up the mess with hose and paper towels.

emotional reactions as he realizes that his playing in mud is being given approval.

Pencils

Kindergarten-size pencils to use for scribbling should be available along with the other classroom supplies.

Result: The child develops the smaller muscles of his hand and fingers. Through pencil scribbling, he becomes further aware of his ability to control linear design. He learns to confine some of his movements to a small area. His visual-motor abilities will increase. He grows in self-esteem as he "writes" like older children and adults. He is prepared for the day when he will begin to learn how to really write.

CHAPTER

6

PAINTS

*"Drip. Drip. Drip. Yellllllllllloooooooooow. Yel——
llllll——ooowwwwwww. Drip it. Drip it. Drip it." Here
was music coming from three-and-a-half-year-old
Lynne as she was immersed in her own private world
of color. I had been teaching for several years. I was
developing ideas on creative teaching, but I didn't
yet understand. For I intruded on that little girl's
world and said, "What a beautiful song. We'll all help
you sing it." I cleverly gathered several children
around me and asked them to join with me in singing,
"Drip. Drip. Drip. Yellllllllllloooooooooow. Yel——
llllllllll—owwwwwwww. Drip it. Drip it. Drip it." Some
of the children joined in. But my little friend, my
creator of songs, did not. With a disinterested shrug,
she put down her paint brush, left her paper, and
walked away. Soon she was sitting in the boat,
seeking solace from the soothing effect of its rhythm
as it rocked to and fro.*

The painting experience enables the child to wander into far-away,
undiscovered lands. As he confronts the painting surface with
his color-saturated brush, his imagination begins to soar. As he
begins to apply the paint, and as his emotions begin to interact
with the medium, the outside world and the people around him
fade into a remote distance. The painting, the color, and the
self become one. Whether the spell is momentary or whether
it lasts for several minutes, the experience refreshes the spirit
and the mind, providing a basis for communication which is not
dependent on verbalization.

Painting can be so important an influence in the overall growth
of the developing child that much care should be taken in the
selection and presentation of the painting materials. Tempera
paint is probably the most satisfactory type of paint for all-around
general use by the child. It is a very easy medium to control.
Since it is water soluble, its density can be varied by the amount

of water or other liquid added to it. One color can be readily mixed with another to produce new colors. Tempera paint is opaque, which permits the child to cover one color with another, thus making changes well within his control. It dries quickly and once dried, it can be painted over. It combines well with other media, allowing for much diversity of use. In addition, using tempera paints enables the child to develop skills that he can apply to many other types of paint and art media.

In purchasing tempera paints, consider a fairly good quality in order to give the child the full benefit of the richness and beauty of good paint. However, some of the more expensive types are difficult to wash out of clothing, and may even stain the hands. Avoiding these kinds as much as possible will make the painting experience more acceptable to the child and to his parents as well.

Start out with red, blue (ultramarine or medium), yellow, orange, green, violet, black, and white. If your budget allows, add turquoise blue, magenta, red orange, and yellow green too. Although these colors can be mixed from the basic colors given above, the tempera will not have the same brilliance as the commercially prepared paints.

During the early months of the school year, use your paints as they are. Later on, you can begin to mix many of your own colors to use with the pure colors or to use in place of them. Don't be afraid to experiment. To produce new colors, begin by adding very small quantities of one color to another. Increase the amounts as needed. It is better to add the darker color *to* the lighter one.

Browns.   Red, blue, and yellow make brown. Mix in equal parts, then add more of any one of the colors as needed to get the particular shade of brown you desire. Any two complementary colors also make brown. Thus, green (which is a combination of blue and yellow) and red make brown. Yellow and violet make brown. Other combinations you can use are orange and blue, red orange and turquoise, and magenta and yellow green. Black and red will give a deep brown. You may need to add a touch of green or yellow to get the desired color.

Greens.   Vary your greens by adding blue for blue green, or yellow for yellow green. Make blue green by starting with blue and adding just enough yellow to give the greenish tinge you are seeking. Make yellow green by starting with yellow and adding just a slight amount of blue, gradually, until you have the desired intensity.

Black added in minute quantities to yellow will make chartreuse. Black added in minute quantities to green will give a deep green. You may need to add small amounts of blue or yellow (or both) to get the desired color.

If you add white to make a light green, add some additional yellow to strengthen the color. Add traces of violet to green to gray the color down. This mixture can then be mixed with varying quantities of white for interesting gradations.

Reds. Add traces of blue to your red to give a deep carmine effect. Add traces of black to red, and very small quantities of yellow, for an unusual grayed effect. Vary the value with the addition of white. Also try it without the yellow. Orange mixed with red will make a better red orange than yellow mixed with red. Orange mixed with magenta will make a vivid red.

Blues. Blues can be varied greatly by adding traces of yellow or green. Small amounts of magenta added to blue can give it a greater intensity without changing the color. Blue mixed with small amounts of black and orange will give an interesting grayed effect. Vary with the addition of white.

Yellow. Vary slightly by adding white and traces of orange. Vary slightly by adding traces of black. Gray it by adding traces of violet.

Orange. Vary by adding yellow or red. Gray it by adding traces of blue. Black may be added and so can white. Vary by adding minute amounts of blue and red. Magenta added to orange can produce a luminous red orange.

Violet. Add magenta, blue, or red to vary the color. Add blue and white to get a luminous lavender. Add traces of green and black for a gray effect. Vary with white.

Black. If you have no black paint, mix red, blue, and green for a substitute.

Liquid Tempera

Many companies produce ready-mixed liquid tempera of school quality which is inexpensive to buy and easy to use. These paints vary greatly in texture, brilliance, and lasting power. Try several brands before ordering large quantities of any one brand. If you use liquid tempera, be sure to provide powdered tempera too, so that the child may learn to mix his own paint.

Powdered tempera can be mixed to the same brilliance and creamy consistency of the better liquid temperas. It works best if you add the tempera powder to the water rather than the other way around, for this requires less mixing. To mix powdered tempera, simply follow these five steps:

1. Decide on the amount of paint to be mixed.
2. Fill a container with water equal to one-third the amount of paint desired.
3. Add two-thirds the amount of powdered tempera to the water. *Do not mix.*
4. Let the mixture stand several hours or overnight until the water has soaked up the powdered tempera.
5. After the paint has been well absorbed by the water, stir. It should be somewhat creamy. Add more water or more powdered tempera if necessary.

The thinner the paint, the duller its intensity. Mixed too much or too briskly, tempera, especially colors containing reds, may lose its brilliance. A few drops of alcohol added to the liquid will help these colors mix more readily. Stir all paints as little as possible to prevent oxidation of the pigments. Add a little liquid starch to the mixture to make it more creamy and to extend its use. Too much starch may cause the paint to flake off when dry.

Storing Paint

When you are mixing large batches of powdered tempera, add a few drops of oil of cloves or wintergreen. Otherwise the paint will sour in just a few days, especially if it is stored in covered containers. Adding a teaspoonful of cologne or alcholol per pint of tempera will also prevent souring. If milk has been added, the paint should be refrigerated when not in use. If the paint is not going to be used for a few days, keep the containers covered to keep it from drying out. Use aluminum foil or Saran Wrap if the containers do not have lids.

Water can also be used as a cover for paint. If you have a container that is about half full of paint, fill it almost to the top with water before storing it, whether covered or left open. Don't mix the water into the paint until the next time you use it. At that time, you can judge the consistency of the mixture by first pouring off most of the surface water and then stirring the paint with a brush. Storing paint in this way will keep it from caking at the bottom of the container. However, by preparing only the amounts needed for one or two days at a time, the containers can be washed frequently and you will have no caking and storage problems. Always keep paint in as cool a place as possible.

Containers

The traditional empty milk carton used as paint container neither adds to the attractiveness of the environment nor to the anticipation of the activity. Milk cartons may be expedient for use in large classes of elementary school children, but have no place in the nursery school. When you select paint containers you should consider their aesthetic as well as practical qualities. Glass containers, although attractive, are not desirable because of their breakability. Clear plastic containers that let the color show through are as attractive as glass ones and are safer to use. Empty frozen juice cans also make good containers for paint. The smallest size is just right for two-year-old hands, and the larger ones are easily handled by four- and five-year-olds. A good in-between size is the Awake can, which also has a re-usable plastic lid.

When preparing cans for use as containers for tempera paints, paint them in bright enamel colors to match the color of the paint that will be used in them. I usually prepare three 12-ounce cans for each color used in classes with four-, five-, or six-year-olds. One or two 6-ounce frozen juice cans of each color are enough for groups of two- to three-year-olds, depending on how many are painting at one time.

First, cover the outside surface of the can with a metal undercoater, which can be sprayed on. Next, paint the can with one coat of enamel in the desired color. If the desired color of enamel is not available, paint the can with tempera. To make the mixture waterproof, add approximately one-half as much canned milk as you have liquid paint. The can may later be sprayed with several coats of plastic to give an enamel-like appearance. Prepare a number of extra cans in plain white or black for new color mixtures, seasonal colors, and other uses.

Brushes

Easel brushes are commonly used for tempera painting. Provide several sizes and kinds. The handles should usually be long for greater freedom of use and to encourage greater movement.

However, you can cut two inches off the ends if the brushes are to be used with small-sized juice cans by two-year-olds.

Brush handles may be unpainted soft wood or either lacquered or highly polished hardwood, the latter being more expensive. Try to buy brushes that are set in seamless aluminum or nickel-plated ferrules (holders). Brush ends may be made of bristle (hog hair), squirrel hair, badger, ox hair, or sable. Bristle brushes are most commonly used because they are the least expensive and some educators think a young child should only use stiff brushes. When you buy bristle brushes, be sure to obtain those with the longer bristles. Brushes that are flat and long are called *flats*. Those which are rounded and tapered are called *rounds*. Both types should be provided in fairly large sizes (¾" to 1").

In addition to your supply of bristle brushes, provide the children with some good quality brushes of squirrel hair or other flexible hairs. These should include both flats and rounds, but can be slightly smaller than the bristle brushes (½" to 1"). They will greatly enhance the experiences of children in their painting activities because they hold a large quantity of paint and are very flexible. In purchasing these soft-haired brushes, remember that camel hair is not too satisfactory for tempera painting, but is fine for use with watercolors.

Sponges

Sponges of all types and sizes encourage the child to experiment whenever you give them to him together with small dishes of tempera paint and a surface to paint on.

Rollers

Provide the type of paint rollers commonly used for finishing work in house painting. These are available in different shapes, widths, and textures. You can make interesting new textures for your paint rollers by covering them with such things as net, mesh, velvet, hopsacking, or dotted swiss. Try strips of two or three different textures on one roller. Place paper and rollers on a table top or on the floor. Provide one or two containers of color for each of the rollers being used. Small cookie trays, baking pans, or similar flat containers are satisfactory for holding the paint.

Result: The child practices making and controlling elbow and arm movements. He develops awareness of textural differences.

Three different types of paint rollers and three different colors of paint provide Carole (4) with a challenging experience.

He heightens his concept of cause and effect as he observes that his moving the roller produces marks on the paper.

Feather Dusters

Feather dusters make unique painting tools that produce effects far different from any other type of brush. Purchase the bright, colorful drip-dry dusters that are available at grocery stores and variety stores. Prepare paint by first pouring some liquid starch into a large, shallow baking pan until it almost covers the entire bottom of the pan, but not quite. Then select two contrasting colors of liquid or powdered tempera and pour about one-half cupful of each into two diagonal corners of the pan. Select one

Painting with a feather duster enables Dani (3) to cover his paper quickly with little muscular effort.

more color, this time using powdered tempera, and sprinkle it lightly over the liquid starch. We usually use black for one of the corners, and two harmonious colors for the other corner and the powdered paint—for example, turquoise blue and orange, or violet and yellow.

The method of preparing the paint for this activity is purely experimental. Try other ways too. Offer the child combinations of thick paint, thin paint, wet brush, and dry paint. Always keep the paint spread thin in the pan so that the feather duster does not get too wet. After some experimentation with feather dusters, introduce whisk brooms as a painting tool. This will provide a strong contrast to the softness and ease of the feather duster painting. Other household brushes may also be used.

Result: The child finds that he is able to cover the paper very quickly in comparison to working with traditional tools. His feeling of self-importance increases as he observes the power and result of his actions. Since the paint comes off with what seems like a very light touch of the feather duster, the child extends his abilities to understand the cause and effect of his arm movements in relation to muscular exertion. He develops new concepts of space and time as he finds that he is able to cover a given area in a shorter amount of time.

Two Brushes

Sometimes give the child only two colors of tempera and two brushes or feather dusters, one for each hand. Or give him only one color with two brushes. This activity is best done on an easel or on a board propped up for use as an easel.

Variation
- Provide musical accompaniment using various kinds of dance music.

Result: The child further develops his ability to function bilaterally. Visual-motor perception develops as his eyes follow the movements of both arms simultaneously.

Other Painting Tools

Twigs, feathers, Q-tips, squeeze bottles, and anything else your imagination or that of the child hits on can also be used for applying paint to paper.

Painting Surfaces

Easels. You don't *have* to use expensive easels to paint on. You can use table tops, floors, walls, or any other surface that is easy for the child to reach. Given a choice, in fact, most very young children would choose to paint on the floor first, and then standing at a table.

If table tops are used, cover the table with a protective covering. Plastic or oilcloth coverings are commonly used. Newspaper is also a good covering. The important thing is to make the child comfortable by arranging the materials and equipment in a way that will keep him from worrying about making a mess. The table

Large pieces of wall board make good painting surfaces for Marty and Susan (both 5).

should be low enough so that the child can paint with ease from a standing position

Whether you prefer to have the child paint on horizontal surfaces, as I do, or whether you prefer to use easels, be sure to give the child opportunities to experience both methods. Each method provides for a different type of visual excersise and muscular movement, both of which are pertinent to the child's growth and development.

Celotex Painting Boards. I have found that $4' \times 8'$ sheets of Celotex or other kinds of wall board make excellent and versatile surfaces on which to conduct the painting activities. They can be cut into $4' \times 4'$ squares for ease in handling. They can be used on table tops or floors. They can be placed on $4'' \times 6''$ or $6'' \times 8''$ blocks to raise them from the floor. You can stand them against a wall and paint on paper pinned to them as on an easel. Wall board can be carried out-of-doors. Both sides can be used. Also, wall board is inexpensive, so it can easily be replaced from time to time.

When the children are going to paint, you can make them and yourself more at ease by anticipating the possibility of spilled or splattered paint. Provide aprons for teacher and child and protective coverings for table tops, floors, and other objects. Place buckets or dishpans of slightly soapy water nearby for the quick rinsing of hands before regular washing in the lavatory. Have paper towels and sponges nearby for hand rinsing and emergencies. Give the child paper, paint, brushes, and other materials suitable to the type of activity you have planned.

Encourage the child to keep his paint on the left side of his paper, whether he is painting at an easel, on a table top, or on the floor. This helps develop in the child a left-to-right orientation that will be important for reading and writing.

Set the paints out where the child can select the colors as he feels the need for them. There should be a brush in each container of color, and the child should be taught to always replace it in the same container when he is through with it. Usually no directions should be given to the child except those which may be needed to help him understand and control both the materials and his emotions.

Give the child as much freedom of time, movement, and use of the materials as your facilities and supervisory help will allow. Let him paint as many pictures as time and materials will allow.

Additives.   By adding various materials to the paint mixtures from time to time, the painting experience can be extended in a wide variety of ways. Try these for texture:

To make one pint of tempera	*add small amounts of*
Lumpy	Flour (1 Tb; don't stir too much)
Gritty	Sand (½ tsp.)
Slippery	Glycerin (1 tsp.)
Slimy	Thickened liquid soap (2 Tbs.)
Sticky	Karo syrup (2 Tbs.)
Rough	Sawdust (1 Tb.)
Shiny and grainy	Sugar (½ cup)

Add ½ cup of salt to 1 pint of tempera to produce a sparkly effect. Do not add it to the paint, however, until you are ready to use it because the salt dissolves rather quickly. In addition to regular table salt, you may also use large-grained salt such as the kinds used in ice-cream freezers or water softeners. Epsom salts and Kosher salt provide further variations. Epsom salts leave very white marks on dark paper when the paint dries.

Liquid soap added to the paint will make it possible to paint over crayon drawings or other waxy surfaces such as milk cartons, ice-cream containers, and cottage cheese boxes. Add 1 Tb. soap to each pint of tempera. Too much soap will give the paint a cloudy cast when it dries.

Non-toxic wheat paste may be added to tempera in place of liquid soap or detergent to paint over waxy surfaces. Paint with wheat paste in it tends to be transparent. Adding white paint will make it more opaque.

You may also want to add things to your paint to change the odor. To ½ pint of tempera add one of the following: cinnamon (1 tsp.), cloves (a few), allspice (1 tsp.), toilet water (1 Tb.), liquid flavorings such as vanilla or peppermint (½ tsp.), bleach (½ tsp.), ammonia (½ tsp.), or lemon juice (1 Tb.).

What To Do with Tempera Paints

There are many ways to paint with tempera to provide different kinds of learning experiences for the young child. Here are some suggestions.

Free Painting

Provide a selection of colors (varying it from day to day or week to week), paper, and appropriate brushes. The two-year-old should be given only two or three colors to use. The three-, four-, or five-year-old should start out with two or three colors, but these can very soon be increased to five or six. The experienced or older child can be allowed to select from six to eight colors at a time. The child should be reminded to keep each brush in the color of paint it starts out in. Allow him to experiment freely with the materials, to choose colors as he wants, and to brush them on in any way that he enjoys. Watch that he doesn't misuse the brush. Allow him as much time as he needs and let him paint more than one picture if he wants to. Be sure his name is printed on his paper in the upper left-hand corner. This will get him accustomed to looking in the corner, which will be important to him when he begins to learn how to read and write.

Result: The child learns the technique of brush tempera painting. He sets his own standards and begins to realize his own capacities. He learns to discriminate in his choice of materials

Teri (2) grips her paintbrush in a way that will require her to make bold arm movements. Stevie (3½) is able to use a gentler, more mature grip that allows him greater control of the brush.

and in methods of application. He exercises his large muscles and develops eye-hand coordination. He discovers the enormous number of ways he can arrange and vary spatial forms. He develops an aesthetic appreciation of design and color balance. He tries out ideas, tests his skills, and learns to release his emotions and express his feelings.

Drip Pictures

Mix paint slightly thinner than usual, but not watery. Use easels or stand paint boards at a slight angle against a wall to use as easels. Provide large sheets of paper at least 18″ × 24″. Use them vertically. Suggest to the child that he fill his brush with paint and press it hard against the paper to make the paint run down the paper.

Result: The child learns through this experience how to make the paint drip. He figures out that if he doesn't want the paint to drip he should use less paint and less pressure. This self-teaching experience extends his knowledge of cause and effect. He develops temporal concepts as he observes that some colors drip faster than others, depending on the density of the paint. Sometimes the child will call his picture "Rain," especially if it is done on a rainy day. The experience of making Drip Pictures takes the child a step closer to the time when he will want to make representational pictures.

Drop Paintings

Whenever we do Drip Pictures the children also become interested in making Drop Paintings. Here the brush is held over the paper while the child is standing in an upright position. The paint is allowed to drop and splash where it will.

Place very large sheets of paper flat on the floor. Brown wrapping paper or 36" wide butcher paper will do. Protect the floor around the paper with some type of covering. Mix the paint as you did for the Drip Pictures. Provide many colors. Use your largest bristle brushes. The child may drop the paint from the brush any place on the paper. Several children at a time can work on the painting together. *Rule:* When performing this activity indoors, shaking the brush is not allowed.

Result: The child becomes aware of color patterns being formed by dropping and splashing color in one area. After a while he either moves to another area or changes colors with another child. He finds out that more paint will drop from a full brush. He exercises muscular control and patience as he holds the brush over the paper and waits for the paint to drop. He improves his concept of time. He may learn to wiggle the brush with a slight wrist motion to avoid shaking it in a way that will cause the paint to splatter all over. He participates in group planning as the picture nears its finish and he sees that certain areas seem to need more color than others. He becomes aware of the spatial relationships between himself and the other children as he takes care not to splash paint on their shoes or clothing.

Drip Pictures. By learning how to make the paint drip down a vertical surface, Ken and Karen (both 3) will be able to figure out for themselves how to prevent paint from dripping when they do other kinds of painting.

Drop Painting. Anne, Terry, and Terri (all 5) have developed sufficient control of their finger movements to direct the paint where they want it to drop without flicking their wrists and making it splash.

Splatter Painting. Kari, Julie, and Laura (all 4) learn to control their wrist movements to splatter their paints on various parts of the paper.

This activity is the same as Drop Painting, except that it is done out of doors where the paint can be splattered and splashed more freely. It is preferable that the child be barefoot for this experience. Prepare materials as for Drop Painting, providing smaller pieces of paper for just three or four children at one time to use. If you wish, each child can have his own piece of paper.

Many interesting effects can be achieved by first splattering light colors and then splattering dark colors over them—or the other way around. Add a few splashes of white for a good finishing touch. We frequently use our discarded paint boards for this activity and then trade the finished painting for outgrown toys from home. Some parents like to frame the boards and hang them as abstract paintings in their homes.

Result: The child expands his previous experience of Drop Painting. His awareness of color is intensified as the drops of paint splash on one another and intermingle. He increases his awareness of surrounding space as he shakes his brush in an attempt to get the paint on the paper only and not on the surrounding surface. He also increases his awareness of the needs of others as he takes care not to shake paint on children who are working nearby. After this experience, the grass or pavement should be hosed off to wash away the splattered paint.

Oversized Paintings

Occasionally give the child a very large piece of paper to spread out on the floor so he can make oversized paintings. First, spread out newspapers or other floor covering to protect the surrounding surface and to mark off the area for the child. Set the paint and brushes to the left of the paper, and then let the child proceed without giving him specific directions.

Result: The child increases his understanding of whatever shape the paper has been cut in as he relates his movements to the paper. He reacts according to the shape of the paper. Circular paper, for example, seems to inspire a very gentle, relaxed pose. Rectangular paper, with its sharp corners, seems more conducive to rigorous action. As the child attempts to cover the various parts of the paper with paint he encounters problems that he is required to solve as he decides whether to move himself to another side of the paper or whether to reach and stretch across the paper. He increases his visual-motor abilities as he finds the need to reach and stretch. He acquires specific experience that later can be transferred to other activities, such as making a mural, plotting a garden, or laying out an outdoor area for a game. He takes great pride in his finished picture, recognizing that the large size makes it more noticeable. He grows in self-esteem.

Flag Making

Flag Making is a visual-perception exercise that trains the child to work from left to right, as he will be required to do when he learns to read and write. This type of activity is based on the fact that most children will start painting in the wide area of a triangular piece of paper, working toward the narrow end.

Provide pennant-shaped pieces of paper and several containers of paint for the child to use, with a brush in each container. Put the paper down for the child, making certain that the wide end is on his left. Place the paint next to the wide end. If the child moves the paint, make no comment. Pennants can be 8" to 18" wide and 24" to 36" long.

Variations
- Paint on rolls of paper approximately 12" wide, the rolled end to the child's right. This encourages a left-to-right movement as he unrolls the paper to paint on—and on and on.
- The child can also paint on long, narrow strips. The placement of the paint containers will guide him from left to right. These strips can be approximately 6" to 8" wide and 20" to 36" long. In all painting projects try to think in terms of left-to-right movement.

Result: The child usually works from left to right in these situations. He acquires an increased understanding of angles and triangles and will discover that triangles can have many different shapes and sizes. He usually tends to show new creative ideas when he is encouraged to work from left to right, which is ordinarily the opposite of the way he has been working. These new ideas and techniques will lead to a greater understanding of the many possible ways to divide space.

Negative-space Paintings

Negative-space imagination paper can be used with any art activity, but it is especially interesting for painting. Prepare negative space paper by cutting your regular painting paper into free-form

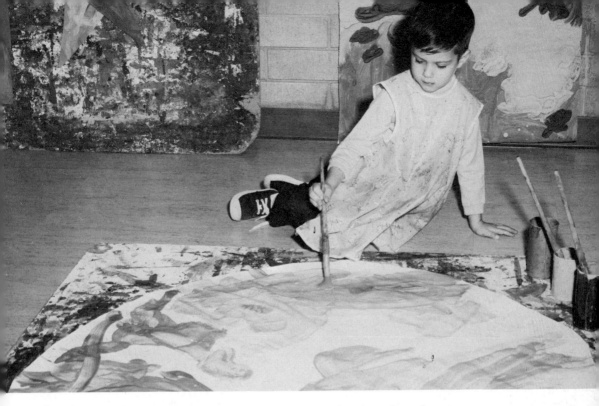

The circular shape of the oversized sheet of paper inspires the relaxed actions by Bret (5) as he explores the space involved. Compare Bret's posture with that of the two children in the picture on page 77.

Flag Making. Chris and Keith (both 5) are handling their brushes in a mature way as they allow the pennant-shaped paper to influence their movements from left to right.

Negative-Space Painting. Peter (3½) is dealing effectively with the problem he encountered by painting on a sheet of paper with a hole in it.

shapes. You can simply cut one, two, three, or all four corners into unusual shapes, or you can make the entire sheet an unusual shape. Cut or tear one or more shapes out of the body of the paper itself. Present the paper to the child without comment. Occasionally he may say his paper is torn or that it has holes in it. Merely tell him that is the kind of paper you prefer that he use that day. Most children will accept this kind of paper as though they used it every day. Negative-space paper can be placed directly on the paint boards, or it can be placed on top of a piece of newspaper in order to make more of a contrast to the child.

Result: The child faces a problem-solving task as he decides how to deal with the negative space on the paper. He learns to think about what he's doing while working since he cannot paint without giving the method some consideration. He improves his muscular coordination because he finds it necessary to give more specific direction to his brush. He becomes more aware of two-dimensional shapes.

Marked Imagination Paper Paintings

Painting on marked imagination paper is similar to painting on negative-space paper except that the motivation is provided by marks on the paper rather than holes cut out of it. Prepare marked imagination paper as described in Chapter 2. Give the paper to the child without comment. If the child wishes to, let him look through all the imagination paper to find a sheet with marks he prefers. He may use the marks on the paper as the taking-off point for a design, or he may ignore them completely. He may use the colors of the marks as the taking-off point for the colors he selects. This is more likely to happen with children who are five and over.

Result: The child's imagination is stimulated by the color, shape, and placement of the marks. He has experience in problem solving as he copes with the fact that his paper already has marks on it. He indicates awareness or lack of it as he notices the marks on the paper or remains completely oblivious of them, as some children do.

Textured Papers

All of the painting activities may be varied by making use of papers that have many different types of textures. Use rough, smooth, or bumpy papers. Use absorbent and nonabsorbent papers. Use heavy papers and thin papers. Use paper that is clear and smooth and paper that is printed or embossed. Experiment with the child to learn which paint mixtures work best on each type of paper.

Result: The child increases his ability to make tactile discriminations.

Making Paint from Basic Ingredients

An important part of the creative art experience is to give the child an opportunity to prepare the paints himself. The secret in setting the stage for this self-directed activity is to provide small quantities of materials. The value is in the complete trust given the child to handle the materials according to his abilities.

Paint-mixing Experiences

On a tray, place clear plastic drinking glasses ⅔ full of powdered tempera, some tongue depressors or plastic or wooden spoons to use for scooping out and mixing the paint, and a small pitcher of water. On a separate tray, nearby but not too close, place some three-ounce paper cups which the child will use to mix the paints in. The small size will help to limit the amount of materials he takes at one time. Keep the brushes and an assortment of paper near the area where the painting will be done. The child may need to be reminded not to let the brush stand in the paper cup because the cup will tip over. Put the cup in a small juice can for added support. At first, the child may just enjoy mixing the paint and not using it on paper at all.

Brandon and Connie (both 4) are completely absorbed in the task of mixing their own tempera paint.

Result: Mixing paint (or any materials) is an excellent visual-motor exercise for the child. He discovers that the more paint he uses, the darker the color gets. He also discovers that it is easier to add a little water at a time to the paint than to darken the color by adding paint to too much water. Thus he develops concepts of proportion and quantity and he increases his ability to control his muscular movements as he learns to control the pouring of the water. He sometimes experiments with mixing two colors together to create a third, and he develops an understanding of his own ability to create and control materials. When he uses the paint he has prepared, he sometimes uses a thin wash over the entire sheet of paper, taking great pride in every brush stroke as he recognizes that he is covering the paper with the same paint that he created. More frequently, however, he creates very careful color arrangements, taking extra care in keeping the various colors distinct. His pride in having made his own paint becomes evident in the consciousness with which he creates deliberate patterns of line and color in contrast to the more random development of paintings done with paint that someone else has made. This new-found awareness is then transferred to his work with prepared paints and other types of media.

Paint-making Experiments

After the child has had considerable experience painting with tempera, give him an opportunity to experiment with making various new mixtures of his own. Prepare several containers of paint to be shared, medium-size pieces of painting paper, and stiff bristle brushes that can be used for mixing. Give each child several small mixing pans. We use disposable aluminum muffin tins, divided into four sections for each child. Small jars, paper cups, cottage cheese cartons, and similar containers can serve the same purpose. Allow the child to select various cleaning materials and other household products to use in the experiments. Let the child make suggestions. Place all materials in the center of the working area, preferably on a lazy Susan for convenience in sharing. Have the child place in his pan small amounts of any color he chooses. He then selects any ingredient he wishes from the lazy Susan and mixes it with one of his colors of paint. Then he tries the resultant mixture out on paper and discusses the results with the other children and you. Because the discussion is an important aspect of this activity, it calls for closer supervision than in most other art experiences.

These 4- and 5-year-olds, with the help of a visiting father, are adding kitchen cleanser, toothpaste, hand lotion, and liquid soap to liquid tempera. They will compare their mixtures and discuss the results. The discoveries they make during this activity are especially important because they are *their own.*

Ingredients To Use	Probable Result
Toothpaste	Transparent, easy to mix, smells good.
Cold cream, face cream	Greasy, doesn't mix.
Hand cream	Hard to mix, but can be done.
Hand lotion	Good smell, semi-transparent.
Liquid soap (old and thickened)	Slimy, very transparent.
Kitchen cleanser	Powdery when dry, opaque, dull finish.
Salad oil	Hard to mix, oily.
Catsup or mustard	Nauseating to adults, fun for the child.

Also use other additives that you think would be effective for textural differences and odors. To extend the activity, actually use the paint for making pictures.

Result: The child acquires experience in scientific experimentation and planning. He increases his ability to discriminate between odors, textures, effects, and similar qualities of the mixture, as well as his ability to judge quantities. He practices verbal evaluation of his experience. He develops muscular control and decision-making skills as he learns to regulate amounts.

Whipped Soap

Whipped soap can be made with either soap or detergent. Soap, however, retains the color in the foam better and is far more satisfactory. It is easier to clean up, too. Soap flakes give a better texture than powdered soap.

Provide a pitcher of water, a container to mix the soap in, an egg beater, and the soap. Give the child some food coloring or tempera to mix into the whipped soap. He will also need paper and brushes. Sponges or other painting tools may also be used.

The child makes the whipped paint himself. First he pours

Mark and Terri (both 5) make whipped soap paint while Jaqui and Jo-Jo (both 4½) watch.

water into the mixing bowl or container and then he adds soap flakes. He beats the soapy water with the egg beater until the mixture is frothy, but not stiff. (If the soap gets too stiff, it will be difficult to use because it may be too slippery to apply. Also, it will crack when dry.) He stirs color into the beaten soap slowly. Colors will usually be pale.

Use whipped soap for general experimental painting activities. Without color added, whipped soap can be used to achieve the effect of snow. It is also good for decorative effects on borders, boxes, and designs. It can be applied with a sponge for special decorative effect.

Result: The child develops the ability to measure and to judge quantities. He increases his scientific knowledge as he observes the action of the mixture as it becomes frothy and as he sees how the mixture toughens as it dries on paper or some other surface. He increases his aesthetic awareness as he experiences involvement with the delicate pastel tints which he has created. He also increases his ability to control his arm movements as he performs the action that causes the eggbeater to work.

Butterfly Blots

Butterfly Blots are more commonly known as ink blot pictures, but we find that the children prefer to call them Butterflies. This is an excellent quick activity for large groups, parties, short sessions, rainy days, and for many other occasions when you want the child to produce something to take home. The child drops wet paint on one half of a sheet of paper. Then he folds the paper in half and blots the wet half with the dry side to produce a mirror image. Provide paper that can be folded easily. Start out with paper that is about half the size you usually give the child to paint on. After the child has had some experience with the activity, use whatever size of paper you wish. Colored construction paper is very effective, and black can be very dramatic with this technique. Prepare several colors of paint that are creamy enough to be rich in color, but just thin enough for it to drop off the brush with the slightest amount of encouragement. *Hints:* Too many colors will cause the design to lose it effectiveness. Adding drops of white after all other colors have been used helps to set off the contrast of the other colors.

Each child folds the paper in half—with your help if it is needed. One introductory method is for you to fold many sheets of paper at once, not creasing them, and then give one piece to each child.

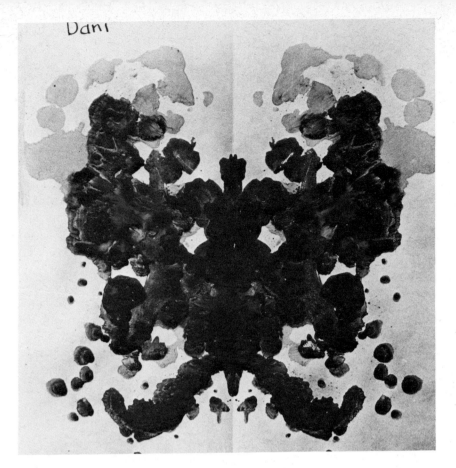
Dani

A Butterfly Blot.

The child may then crease along the fold that has already been suggested. Show the child how to match the edges and corners. The child drops one color on one side of paper in blots here and there. Then he folds the paper over and rubs it with his hand. Then he opens the paper, drops another color, and repeats the process. He folds and rubs after adding each new color.

Variations
- Use mustard or catsup dispenser bottles to squeeze out the paint.
- Use very thin paint on slick-surfaced paper.
- Use rough-textured paper.
- Sometimes add all colors at once, then fold.
- Use different types of color combinations—for instance, several shades of blue and green; red, orange, yellow, and black; black and white only; primary colors only; one complementary pair or split-complements only.
- Invent variations of your own.

Result: The child acquires experience in folding paper and learns the concept of halves. He develops further control of the brush as he directs paint over just one half of the paper. He increases his awareness of cause and effect and his awareness of color mixtures and color relationships. He enjoys the experience of anticipation as he folds the paper, rubs it, and then reopens the paper to view the result. He increases his aesthetic appreciation as he becomes aware of the beauty of the symmetrical designs he is creating, which helps him to develop a concept of symmetry. He learns to follow a definite sequence of steps in making a design.

Blurred Folds

An experience that is similar to Butterfly Blots and also good to use for short or special sessions is that of forming a symmetrical design by pulling painted string between two pieces of paper. Use creamy tempera paint, medium-sized paper, and lengths of string or yarn. The paint will be blurred.

The child folds and creases a piece of paper, preferably lengthwise. Then he dips a piece of string or yarn into paint. He places it on one side of the paper and folds the other side over it. Holding one hand on the paper over the string, the child pulls the string out through one end of the fold. The result is a symmetrical design formed by the string smearing the paint on the paper. The child should use only one string at a time.

Variation

- Use three related colors, such as red, red orange, and orange, to achieve subtle variations as one string blends the paint into the pattern made by another.
- Use a string to apply one color and a piece of thick yarn to apply another color. Pull them both through the paper at the same time.
- Use two primary colors to form a third color as the two are blended together.
- Achieve different effects by using narrow strips of very thin wood, narrow strips of cloth, a piece of lace, a green twig.

Result: The child experiences great anticipation to see the result of his action. He increases his awareness of cause and effect. He increases his knowledge of elements of design and the meaning of symmetry. He also learns the meaning of *blurred*. He gains experience in following a sequence of three steps.

After using string for making Blurred Folds, the child may want to experiment with other types of string painting. Provide a wide variety of types and lengths of strings and yarns. The child first dips the string into a small dish of tempera paint, and then drags the string across the paper to make various designs. Or he may want to hold the the string vertically and let it drop onto the paper—how it falls determines the design. A mixture of equal parts liquid starch and liquid tempera can be used for this activity. The string or yarn is allowed to dry on the paper. The starch will cause it to adhere, making a three-dimensional design.

Result: The child will extend his knowledge of the physical world as he experiments with the string and the paint.

Ben, David, and Todd (all 4½) are making string paintings. This activity is set up in a way that permits the child to pursue it completely on his own terms without teacher direction.

Additional painting experiences can be attained through the variation of ways of presenting the materials. Here are some ideas.

Wet Paper

Wet the paper thoroughly before use, blotting any puddles with a sponge. Drop paint on the paper or apply it directly with a brush, allowing the colors to run together.

Variations
- Crumple the paper before wetting it. Colors will not only blend together, but will be emphasized in the lines formed by the wrinkles.
- Use watercolor instead of tempera.
- Use eye droppers and food coloring mixed with water or full strength.
- Sprinkle powdered tempera from salt shakers on *very* wet paper. Use colors that blend well.

Result: These experiments extend the child's knowledge of the design possibilities in the interaction of paint and water. He develops a concept of *wrinkled* and discovers that he may not always be able to control the designs that he creates.

Dry Paint

Reverse the experience described above by using dry paint with wet brushes. The child can experiment first with dry paper, and then with wet paper. Or he can use paint that has not been mixed thoroughly, so that the brush carries some dry powdered tempera along with the wet. The child can experiment with applying the dry tempera to wet paper with cotton balls or a wad of wet facial tissue instead of brushes. Powdered tempera sprinkled from a salt shaker onto wet paper produces an interesting design. The child may want to use a brush to spread it out. These variations can be done at separate times or they can be combined into one project.

Result: The child increases his knowledge of the differences between wet and dry. He heightens his appreciation of the visual impact of pure color. This introduction to processes that can be reversed encourages his imaginative use of materials and techniques.

Drop very runny paint on the paper. The child picks up the paper and tilts it from side to side and back and forth to form designs as the paint runs. Provide fairly small, easy-to-handle sizes of paper.

Result: The child's awareness of gravity is enhanced.

Blowing Color

Blow the paint around the surface of the paper with straws rather than tilting the paper. Be sure that the straws are wide and that the paint is quite runny.

Result: The child increases his understanding of air movement as he realizes he can control that movement to force paint into interesting designs.

Squeezing Color

Apply the paint from squeeze bottles like those which catsup and other household supplies come in. The paint should be creamy.

Result: Squeezing the bottles helps develop the child's control of the small muscles in his hands and fingers.

Dipping Color

Fold very absorbent paper towels or cleansing tissues into four parts. Dip each corner into a container of thin paint. When the child opens the paper he will find that the colors have intermingled with one another to make an interesting symmetrical design.

Variations
- Cut small holes in each corner of the towel or tissue before dipping it. This is an easy beginning project for cutting folded paper.
- Another way to do this experiment is to dip the corner of a folded paper towel into red, blue, yellow, and green food coloring. Open the paper. When it is dry, the colors will have separated into their original four colors.

Result: The child is encouraged to experiment. He develops an understanding of the concept of absorbency and an aesthetic appreciation of symmetry.

The key to effective, creative teaching is to watch for clues in the behavior of the child and to respond to those clues for his. benefit. You will increase your understanding of the child's needs by noticing such things as how he moves while handling his brush and how his facial expressions change as he unfolds his paper to see the symmetrical design of a Blot Picture. Observe his excitement as he experiments with materials. Share his pride in his ability to manipulate the tools. Cushion his disappointment if he temporarily loses control of the materials. Try to recognize his emotional needs and help him to release his tensions.

Tell the child that everyone has moods, that they vary from time to time, and that he should feel free to express *his* moods. Moods are important keys to understanding the child as an individual. Experimenting with mood paintings will help him understand what moods are. This activity helps him to verbalize and act out his feelings. The weather makes a good starting point in experimenting with mood paintings. Ask the child to try to put into a painting how he feels about the weather outside. Later, discuss his painting with him and ask him if he has any ideas or feelings of his own that he would like to express in another painting.

Foggy Day Mood

Provide paper, brushes, and black and white paint. Experiment with white paper and with blue paper. Discuss which kind of paper makes the black and white paint look more like a foggy day.

Variations
- Use sponges instead of brushes.
- Use chalk on dark paper.
- Apply the paint with cotton balls.

Sunny Day Mood

Provide light blue paper and yellow and white paint. Discuss how the sun makes you feel. Provide a selection of papers and paints. Discuss the sun, warmth, and accompanying feelings. Suggest that the child pick out the kinds of colors and paper that make *him* feel like the sun.

Let the child select paper, paints, and any other materials he needs to make a "happy" picture. An older child may want to paint clowns. Let him begin by painting a sheet of newspaper with an overall coat of white paint. When the white paint is dry, allow the child to select any colors he needs to finish the picture.

Night Mood

Let each child decide on materials needed for painting *night*. All of the suggestions should be discussed and varied to suit your own mood and the general tenor of your class.

Representational Paintings

The young child does not *need* to be given subject matter to paint. The painting materials and the manner in which they are presented to him are motivation enough. As the child experiments with and reacts to the wide variety of materials you offer him, he develops concepts of color, balance, rhythm, and design. He learns to sense just where to put the next brush stroke, the contrasting color, the curved line. He may choose the color that is closest to him, or he may carefully pick out those colors that reflect his mood or his sense of design.

Paintings by the young child communicate much in the way of feelings, expression, and reaction to the environment. The child senses this communication as he notes the expression on his mother's face when she sees his newest painting or as he notes the care with which you mount and display his painting. If the activities have been kept within his level of ability, if he has been accorded true freedom in their pursuit, he himself has grown richer in all areas of development.

The five-year-old child eventually develops the desire to communicate through representational painting. You may then occasionally want to suggest some subject matter that relates to a class activity or study, or let him use his own imagination. Caution must be taken to *encourage only,* and not to *direct.* To inspire artistic achievement is your task; to discover his own creative abilities is the task of the child himself. He must be allowed to represent things in his own way, with his own idea of perspective or lack of it, at his own pace, and in his own style. If your motivation takes him off on an unexpected tangent, learn to applaud his originality and to appreciate his self-direction. Listen to him and learn about the unexpected ways of the imagination of a child. This is creativity. Listen to him and allow your own self to grow.

Fingerpainting

Smearing mixtures with his fingers is not a new kind of experience to the child, but by the time he reaches nursery school it has become a repressed art. When fingerpainting is presented to him as a school experience, he frequently approaches it with great caution. He does not quite understand why, after being told so many times to keep his hands clean, the teacher is encouraging him to get them dirty. If he continues to balk, the teacher must be very patient and gentle and she must give him plenty of time to decide to participate. When he hears the word "soap," his fears are lessened. (Mothers like soap.) A small amount of a very light color, such as yellow, added to liquid soap can help to convince the child that he will not be punished for fingerpainting. One or two such experiences are usually all that are necessary before the reluctant child is ready to use the regular paints like the other children.

The basic materials for fingerpainting activities are, of course, paint and a surface to smear it on. Provide some commercially prepared paint. Vary it with starch fingerpaint, wheat paste, liquid starch, library paste, paste fingerpaint, or liquid soap. Use tempera paint or add food coloring to color the ingredients.

For the painting surface, I prefer butcher paper to commercial fingerpaint paper. It is usually of better quality. A good quality 80 lb. drawing paper can also be used. You can also try waterproof wallpaper, drawer lining paper, or a smooth-finished cardboard, such as tagboard. If paper or cardboard with a smooth surface is not available, your available paper or cardboard may be sprayed with a light coat of clear plastic. To keep the paper from curling as it dries, fold each side of each sheet of paper about 1″ from the edge, or simply iron the reverse side of the paper when it is dry.

Surfaces other than paper or cardboard are also suitable for fingerpainting. Try smearing the paint directly on an oilcloth or formica table top, for example. The use of such surfaces can encourage the child to paint more freely, since he is not limited by the size of a piece of paper. Monoprints, described on page 104, may be taken from these surfaces to preserve the design.

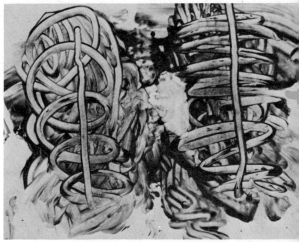

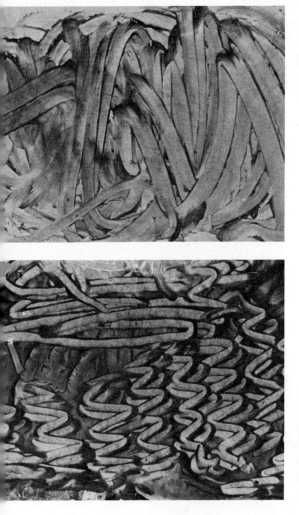

There is considerable variation and individuality in these fingerpaintings as well as evidence of a developing sense of rhythm, balance, and symmetry, indicating that the child is learning to function in a bilateral manner. Fingerpainting is one of the most important types of art experiences for the young child. It has a wholesome influence in the affective and cognitive areas of his development.

Mary (4) and Tom (5) introduce fingerpainting to their brother, Stephen (2). In creative developmental art, the child is always able to help younger children because each child learns the basic procedures required for each activity.

Cooked starch, choice of dry or liquid tempera, and an oversized piece of butcher paper fastened to the ends of the table give Jamie (4) an opportunity for full arm movement as he fingerpaints to music. This experience lasted 20 minutes.

Fingerpainting is usually done while standing at a table. The table should be low enough (18″ to 20″ high) to encourage movement of the entire body as it picks up the rhythm of the arm and hand activity. Enough space should be allowed to ensure that one child's movements do not interfere with the freedom of another child's movements.

Conducting the Activity

Provide aprons for teacher and child. Place protective coverings on areas where they are needed. Have a bucket or dishpan of slightly soapy water nearby so the children can rinse their hands. Place paper towels next to the pail for hand drying and for emergency cleanups. Kitchen sponges are also useful.

Wet the paper for each child before he uses it. Dipping it in water, or wetting the table with a sponge before putting the paper down, and then sponging the paper, are two common methods. Wetting the surface underneath prevents slipping. If liquid soap or liquid starch is used, the surface of the table need not be wet in advance.

Set out the fingerpaint in several containers to allow the child a free choice of colors. Provide spoons with which to scoop up the paints. The teacher should do this for the beginner. The child will do it for himself when he feels he is ready. The child who is familiar with fingerpainting can simply scoop out the paint with his hands. Use attractive, neat containers such as plastic or glass bowls, refrigerator storage containers, or aluminum sauce pans. Encourage the child to paint with the entire palm of each hand, as well as his fingers, wrists, arms, and elbows. Encourage him to move as much as possible. A simple suggestion, such as, "You can cover the whole paper," may encourage the reluctant child to move more freely. When he has finished, help the child place his picture in a special area to dry.

Occasionally add *liquid starch* or *buttermilk* to the paint. Put it in small plastic pitchers or bottles so that the child can handle it himself. The child can also fingerpaint with a mixture made by sprinkling *dry tempera powder* onto liquid starch or buttermilk that he has spread over his paper. (The blue color of the liquid starch may alter the tempera colors somewhat, especially white, yellow, orange, and red.) Advise the child to use the tempera powder sparingly because too much of it will cause the mixture to become opaque.

The child can also make Sticky Painting by adding a small

amount of *Karo syrup* to the paint or pouring it directly onto the paper. He can make Gooey Painting by putting a spoonful of *vegetable glue* in the middle of the paper and spreading it around with the paint. He can make Lumpy Painting by adding *lumpy starch* or a mixture of *lumpy flour and water* to the paint. He can make Sandy Painting by putting a teaspoonful of *sand* into the paint.

Pudding Painting

Pudding Painting should be offered to the child at least once during each school year. Instead of paint, prepare a large quantity of several flavors of pudding. Add some whipped cream if you wish. Use a clean oilcloth or table top to paint on. Suggest that the painting be limited to hands and fingers. Save wrists, arms, and elbows for another time. The hands can be licked before washing.

Mud Painting

Mud Painting can be a real highlight. Add some liquid soap and liquid starch to mud to increase its transparency. For a special treat, make mud handprints all over an outside window that can later be washed off with a hose.

Monoprints

Provide tempera paint that has a little glycerin added to it. Allow the child to fingerpaint on a plastic table top, plastic board, or oilcloth. When the child has finished painting, place a sheet of drawing paper over the painting and then remove it with a quick upward motion. The fingerpainting will be reproduced on the paper, resulting in a Monoprint that preserves the child's design.

Variations
- Fingerpaint on textured paper. The child can create his own textured paper by pasting a variety of torn paper shapes all over a sheet of paper. As he smears the paper with his fingers and hands, feeling the textures of the torn edges, he will experience increased sensitivity to the fingerpainting activity.
- Fingerpaint on crayoned paper, which should be prepared in advance. The crayon underneath the fingerpaint produces a somewhat luminous effect.
- Make handprints on paper tablecloths. These are great for use on a refreshment table for a parents' meeting.

Result: The child's early tactile memories, which he has been forced to repress, are reawakened, providing basic inner satisfactions. His visual perception is increased. Fingerpainting provides direct physical interaction and kinesthetic experience and it stimulates the child's awareness of the concepts of color and transparency. It provides ego strength as the child learns that he can control the paint. The rhythmic movement and sensory experience provide avenues for the free expression of feelings and healthy emotional release, and the good feelings that accompany fingerpainting open the way to increased social growth.

Footpainting

Footpainting can be an interesting warm-weather experiment and is an excellent exercise for building body image. Spread large sheets of paper on the floor. Pour a small quantity of buttermilk onto the paper. Add approximately one-half teaspoon of liquid tempera. The child then removes his shoes and socks to paint barefooted on the paper. The surface will be very slippery, so the child should not stand up on the paper. He can sit in a chair at the edge of the paper and manipulate the paint with his feet.

The child can also make a Butterfly with his feet. While the child holds your hand, he carefully makes footprints by crossing his feet so that the left foot is on the right side and vice versa. The resulting image looks something like a butterfly. But more important, the child can challenge people to tell him what is "wrong" with the picture. It takes most adults a little time to realize that the footprints are reversed. The child can also make Reversed Handprints. The result will look as though the print had been made by the backs of the hands.

Result: The child increases his sensory awareness. This activity also helps to release the remnants of any inhibitions stemming from early repressions. It also increases his awareness of self and of body image, and it promotes imaginative use of media.

Organic Fingerpainting

Organic Fingerpainting is a very effective basic learning experience. Provide a variety of ingredients in their original containers or in pitchers or bowls. Include liquid starch, library paste, hand lotion, vegetable glue, shaving cream in an aeresol can, cooked starch, dry wheat paste, cake flour, and similar materials. Let your own imagination guide you in discovering new ingredients

Organic Fingerpainting. Julie and Ian (both 4) are experimenting with adding salad oil, liquid starch, wheat paste, hand lotion, and shaving cream to their fingerpaint. They are free to use these materials in their own way.

to use. Also provide several small pitchers of water, small containers of powdered tempera, and paper, as you do for other fingerpainting projects. Allow the child to select colors and ingredients as he wishes. Provide tongue depressors for use in scooping up the powdered color. This will help limit the quantities used, preventing opaqueness.

Result: As the child senses the trust shown in him by the teacher, he develops his own sense of trust in others. He experiences the results of his own choices and his own actions. His concepts of basic scientific principles are increased. The complete freedom of choice which accompanies this type of activity builds self-confidence and increases the child's ability to withstand the emotional pressures of highly structured situations he may later encounter.

Fingerpainting is actually a rhythmic movement experience, and it can be enhanced through the use of music. Once the child has become thoroughly familiar with fingerpaint and has had plenty of time to explore its possibilities and develop his own style, music can add a completely new dimension.

Because any rhythmic movement activity should be based on the child's natural movements, it is important that the child be able to work with the material on his own terms and with his own movements before you add musical accompaniment.

Start with a gay waltz, such as "The Skater's Waltz" or "The Blue Danube." Then try a folk dance, such as "Round and Round the Village" or "Here We Go Round the Mountain." Most children prefer fast music and they like it to be loud. Tell them they can rinse off their hands whenever they want to, dance a while, and then go back to their painting.

On another day, use a tambourine to beat out the rhythm while you improvise a song of your own. Improvised songs may be sung to a familiar tune. For example, try the following lyrics to the tune of "Skip to My Lou."

> My hands slide on the paper two by two.
> My hands slide on the paper two by two.
> My hands slide on the paper two by two.
> Skip to my Lou, my darling.

> I can make a motion, so can you.
> I can make a motion, so can you.
> I can make a motion, so can you.
> Skip to my Lou, my darling.

> Now I'll do another one, you can do it, too.
> Now I'll do another one, you can do it, too.
> Now I'll do another one, you can do it, too.
> Skip to my Lou, my darling.

You may also try "Ten Little Indians":

> One little, two little, three little fingers,
> Four little, five little, six little fingers,
> Seven little, eight little, nine little fingers,
> Ten little fingerpaint marks.

> Five little fingers on each hand now,
> Two little hands that I have, somehow,
> Wrists and arms and even an elbow
> Make little fingerpaint marks.

Result: This multisensory experience helps the child to improve his overall muscular control so that he can move more rhythmically while he develops the bilateral coordination of his entire body. He sharpens his auditory perceptual and visual-motor abilities. He experiences a release of tensions as he reacts to the kinesthetic sensations produced by the blending of paint, paper, movement, and music.

Watercolor Painting

Children especially enjoy using watercolors when they are given good quality, *semi-moist* paint to work with. Watercolors are transparent with a sparkle that gives them a clean, fresh look. The colors are easily intermixed. The paint boxes, usually small and individual, are comfortable to use. They offer a satisfying change of pace for the child who has had many opportunities to work with tempera paints.

Watercolor painting is usually done while seated at a table or on the floor. The child's range of movement is confined to a smaller area than when he works standing at a table or an easel, so provide him with smaller sizes of paper. This is a good time to make use of your 9″ × 12″ white drawing paper, scraps of paper left over from larger cut sheets, and the odds and ends of miscellaneous paper accumulated over a period of time. White paper should be used to take optimum advantage of the transparency of the paint. Watercolors are available in sets of four, six, eight, twelve, and sixteen colors. Since we use these paints with the young child for experimentation and sensory training rather than for the promotion of technical skills, I prefer to provide sets with at least eight colors. Provide a good quality brush and a container of water for the child to wash it out in each time he switches to a different color. Show him how to wipe the brush back and forth on a paper towel or cloth after rinsing it in the water. Remind the child to change his water often. You may want to provide him with two jars, one for washing and one for rinsing. Helping the child learn how to keep his brush clean will enable him to respond more freely to the material, since the colors will remain bright and clear. Also suggest to him that "watercolor painting means using lots of water." Then allow him the freedom to do with it what he will.

Sometimes have the the child wet his paper before applying the watercolor. The colors will flow into one another. Occasionally provide the child with two or three pieces of high-quality, profes-

Greg and Alyce (both 4) apply watercolors to paper they have prepared by wrinkling it up and dipping it in water. The colors blend together in unique patterns as they flow into the lines formed by the wrinkles.

sional watercolor paper. These are rather expensive, but can be cut into small pieces, 6″ × 9″ or 8″ × 10″. The pebbly texture of the paper reflects the light and gives the colors an added brilliance.

Result: Painting with watercolors increases the child's aesthetic appreciation of all art because it increases his sensitivity to color, color mixtures, and color combinations. The smaller sheets of paper and the confined working area help him to develop control of his movements. The intimacy of working with his own small set of watercolors also adds to his awareness of himself. He learns to discriminate in what color he selects to use next to another color. He practices following a sequence of directions as he learns about brush washing, care of the paints, and cleaning up. He develops self-confidence because of the ease with which he is able to transfer the colors from the pan to the paper. The child finds beauty in his completed painting and his self-esteem is increased.

A blending of tempera painting techniques and the watercolor experience can be achieved through the use of Tempera Blocks. These are tempera paints that come in cakes of highly concentrated color. The average size of a round cake is approximately 1″ high and 2″ in diameter, or 2″ × 2½″ if rectangular. The colors flow instantly from cake to wet brush and, like watercolor paint, the colors intermix readily. Since the paint is opaque, rather than transparent, the pictorial effect is different from that of watercolors. Paper may be slightly larger than that used for watercolors, perhaps 9″ × 12″ to 12″ × 18″.

PASTES

It's fun to smear paste all over the paper. I'm picking it up just like I saw the teacher doing it. Except she put it on little pieces first. I don't want to bother. I'd rather just put it on my big piece of paper. That gives me more room to smear it around. I wonder why she's making her eyebrows go so funny. She looks like she doesn't like what I'm doing. Yesterday she wanted me to smear black fingerpaint all over the paper. This paste hardly even shows. What's wrong with smearing it like I did the fingerpaint? Oh. I see her smiling now. That's good. Now when she tells me not to eat the paste I'll listen to her. I'll listen because she's learning to let me smear, and that makes me feel good inside. Maybe I'll try sticking on some little circles like she did. Oh, that's the way: Put on some paste, then stick on a piece of paper. Then put on some more paste on top of the little piece and stick another piece on top of that. If I keep doing that I'll have a great big pile right in the middle of my paper. Pasting is fun.

In pasting activities, your goals may not be the same as the child's. Even so, your attitudes toward what he does are important. By allowing the child to explore, you enable him to learn the craftsmanship of pasting. In the beginning, as he familiarizes himself with the material, he must be allowed to get acquainted with it on his own terms. The sensory pleasure derived from smearing is understandable. We realize that the year-old child enjoys squishing and squeezing his cereal or vegetables around in his dish and that he enjoys playing in sand and mud and water. In giving him paste to experiment with, we realize that we are introducing him to another material with which he can satisfy his primitive needs for the manipulation of plastic materials.

While he is smearing and exploring the paste in his early experience with this material, he is gradually refining the use of the smaller muscles of his hands and fingers. This will enable him someday to handle intricate pieces of paper that he has cut himself and to paste them in a deliberate order on a given surface.

Whatever type of paste is used, it should be moist, smooth, and slippery. Fingers are better than brushes for this activity. If you do use brushes, be sure they are clean. Do not give the child a brush that is stuck together with dried paste.

Kinds of Pastes

Ordinary white *library paste* is the best kind for the beginning nursery school student. Open the jar before buying it to make sure it has sufficient moisture to it. If the paste appears to be cracked, try another brand.

Wheat paste is very inexpensive. It can be purchased in powdered form and mixed with water as needed. It is very sticky. Purchase only those brands which are clearly labeled non-toxic. It may attract ants.

Homemade *flour paste* is also a satisfactory medium for pasting. It should be carefully made to avoid lumps. To make it, mix approximately ½ cup of flour with ⅔ cup of water and stir the paste until it has a creamy consistency. Add about ½ teaspoon powdered resin to the mixture and a few drops of oil of peppermint or oil of wintergreen as a preservative. This will make ½ pint.

Cornstarch paste is also good for children's pasting activities. To make it, mix ¾ cup of water, 2 tablespoons light Karo syrup, and one teaspoon white vinegar together in a saucepan and bring the mixture to a full boil. Mix ½ cup of cornstarch with ¾ cup of water and add slowly to the boiled mixture. Stir constantly to avoid lumps. If a few drops of oil of wintergreen are added as a preservative, this paste will be good for about two months. Let the mixture stand overnight before use. This will make one pint of paste.

Other Adhesives

Many other adhesives can also be used. In considering their use, it is good to know that all water-soluable pastes and glues usually cause some shrinkage and warping. Paper that has been pasted or painted with these materials will unavoidably curl. By treating the back of the paper with glue, however, this can be corrected. Some liquid pastes are made especially for paper work and are treated to prevent much of the usual shrinkage and curling.

In her first experience with paste, Andrianna (2½) pasted scraps of paper on top of each other.

White glue is made of vinyl plastic. It is an excellent adhesive. Its use teaches the child the need for careful manipulation of materials. It is much less free a material than "smearing" paste and therefore the child who is using it must manipulate his materials carefully. It dries clear. Use it directly out of its squeeze dispenser bottle, or thin it with water in a small container for use with a brush over large surfaces. It is available in bottles as small as 2 ounces, which you can refill with glue purchased in one-gallon containers.

Rubber cement will not cause shrinkage or curling. It is one of the best adhesives to use with paper. It is especially good to use when mounting pictures for display because they can be pulled off and remounted if straightening is required. Keep a supply of rubber cement solvent on hand to thin out the cement, since it has a tendency to dry and thicken.

Vegetable glue is an excellent substitute for paste. It has the adhering qualities of glue, but can be smeared on with the fingers like paste. Because of its stickiness, it presents valuable tactile experiences for the child. The can must be kept clean, tightly closed, and stored carefully because it attracts ants.

Liquid starch is a good adhesive to use with very thin materials such as tissue paper, napkins, thin cloth, or thread. It may be applied with a paint brush.

Mucilage in a rubber-tipped bottle should be used occasionally to provide yet a different kind of gluing experience.

Tapes. Tapes are also useful material to use in activities that involve sticking things together. Try these:

Masking tape is best for all-around use. It adheres well and it sticks to most surfaces. It is available in bright red and blue as well as the traditional buff.

Cellophane tape is easy for the child to use. Its use provides good exercise for finger muscles.

Gummed Kraft tape is a paper tape that has to be moistened in order to use it. It is not easy for the young child to handle, but it offers a challenging learning experience.

Mystic tape is gummed tape available in both cloth and plastic finish. It comes in many exciting colors and can be used for mending and decorating.

Fastening Devices

Fastening devices can be used in making constructions, collages, and arrangements. Staplers, paper clips, paper fasteners, wire, string, rubber bands, and similar materials may be given to the child to use when needed. These are all excellent manipulatory materials.

Collage and the Arrangement of Space

From his first conscious moments, the child has explored the physical space that surrounds him. He has had various kinds of experiences with the physical objects in his environment, such as the playthings with which he has spent much of his time—on the floor, at tables, in the sandbox, out of doors—and from these experiences he has been developing concepts related to distance, direction, shape, form, and size. He has found that he can fit his toys on certain shelves if he places them a certain way. He has discovered that jigsaw puzzle pieces will fit if the shape of the space they go into is the same as the shape of the piece. He has discovered that he needs to stand on his toes to reach the light switch, and he has learned to fit his foot into the space inside his shoe.

Finished collage projects.

Collage making gives the child the opportunity to extend these learnings to another dimension. He is able to arrange paper and materials from his environment on a flat surface, such as a piece of cardboard or paper. He has the opportunity to stick things together. He can make a design or arrangement by fastening flat materials to one another or to another surface. He can fasten three-dimensional objects and textured materials to a flat surface. This activity gives the child the opportunity to explore, to try out, and to discover things to do with the objects and materials he has at hand. Each time he makes a collage, he has the experience of his previous collages on which to draw. As he is given more and more such opportunities, and he begins to use "found" materials from the environment—materials which help him to interact more directly with that environment—that he can arrange in his own way, he further develops concepts of space, direction, size, and shape. He becomes better able to understand and cope with the physical world.

Collages are made from all kinds of odds and ends, such as interesting pieces of paper, scraps of cloth, plastic, wood, cardboard, old buttons—anything, in fact, that has texture, form, color, pliability, plasticity, flatness, thickness, notches, holes, points, eyelets, transparency, or the wonderful, intriguing quality of being absolutely useless. If you look through your drawers, storage boxes, and wastebaskets, you'll probably find enough items to make any number of collages. But don't stop there. Also check your cupboards, your sewing corner, and your repair supplies. Check your garage, your attic, your cellar. Clean out old toy boxes and save old gift wrappings and greeting cards. Ask for a chance to look through the discards from shops, factories, offices, and stores. Even one day's search will uncover a wealth of material from which you can select exciting materials for collage and constructions.

When you are out of doors—in your own backyard, at the ocean, park or mountain resort, in the country, at the edge of a stream—take a look around and start collecting. You'll find interesting shells and tiny rocks, seeds and pine cones, pine needles and autumn leaves, twigs and straws, interesting pieces of bark and weeds and dried flowers. If something attracts your attention, pick it up. The uninhibited imagination of the child will put it to use. For a definitive listing of suggested materials see the list at the end of this book.

Paper Collage

The simplest and most logical starting place for collage work is with paper. This kind of collage making involves the application of one piece of paper to another. The opportunities for variety, imaginative combinations, and original ideas are limited only by the paper that is available. The projects listed in this chapter are only suggestions from which you can develop your own ideas.

Scraps of construction paper make a good material for beginning collage work. But even scraps need some preparation before they are used. Cut them to workable sizes and provide some variety in color, shape, and size.

Present the materials in an attractive manner. They may be set out on a table in a transparent plastic box or in several boxes, from which each child may take his materials directly. Some of the materials may be set out on a lazy Susan. The materials may be all grouped together, or scraps of different colors may be put in separate containers. Another way to present them is by size—large, medium, and small. Different ways should be used at various times, for each way provides a different type of eye-hand experience and coordination practice.

Present a small quantity of materials at one time. Too many different colors, sizes, and shapes can be as frustrating to the child as no variety at all. Giving the child too little material will keep him from picking and choosing. Giving him too much may hinder his developing the idea of selecting those pieces he prefers rather than just grabbing the first one he comes to. About three or four times as many pieces as each child might be able to use on one collage should be an approximate guide to quantity.

Select a quantity of materials from your paper-scrap boxes. Set the materials in the center of the working area, either in trays made from flat box lids, on a lazy Susan, or in small piles spread around on a large piece of colored paper or oilcloth. Put a sheet of construction paper—white, black, or colored—at each child's place. Use either 9″ × 12″ or 12″ × 18″ sizes of paper for the beginner.

Put a small jar of paste or the lid of a cottage-cheese carton with a small amount of paste in it to the left of each child's place, or provide a container of paste for two or three children to share. Seashells make intriguing individual paste holders. Provide scissors if they are needed. If the child is new to collage making, tell him how to put the paste onto a small piece of paper and press the pasted side down on the large sheet of paper. If he does it wrong at first, leave him alone. He'll soon figure out how to do it through his own experimentation.

Variations
The collage projects suggested in this section follow the same general plan as paper collage. They utilize a cardboard or paper background with colored paper scraps to paste on.
- Dark construction paper background with long, narrow strips of torn white paper to paste on.
- Cardboard background with geometrical shapes cut out of cardboard to glue on.
- Dark blue construction paper background with three shades of lighter blue paper shapes or scraps to paste on.
- Dark blue, dark green, or black construction paper background with yellow, orange, white, and other light-colored paper scraps or shapes to paste on.
- Round-shaped paper background with round shapes of various colors and sizes. Repeat with round shapes of various colors

but only one size. Repeat again with round shapes of only one color but various sizes.

- Triangular-shaped background with triangular shapes to paste on, first the same color and different sizes, and then the same sizes but different colors.
- Pennant-shaped paper background, approximately 6″ wide at the large end and 12″ to 18″ long. Provide squares of descending sizes, starting with 5″, to paste on. Vary this with other geometric shapes differing only in size. For the more experienced child, vary both the sizes and shapes in the same project.
- Narrow lengths of paper, approximately 4″ × 12″, or 16″ × 20″, as a background with very large scraps to paste on. Scraps should be 3″ to 5″ wide.
- Any type of background with pieces that are the same shape and color, but different in size. Vary this with pieces that are the same size and color, but different in shape. Then vary again with pieces that are the same shape and size, but different in color.
- Any type of background with scraps of paper with geometric shapes cut out of them (negative-space shapes).
- Any background with seasonal or holiday color combinations.

The main things to consider in beginning paper collage making are contrasts of sizes, colors, textures, and shapes. These differences in materials will insure interest and promote originality, as well as help the child develop conceptual understandings. After the child has learned the basic technique of pasting, he can learn to tear paper to make original shapes. Later, after he has learned to cut paper, the child may cut his own geometric shapes to use for pasting. The younger child will have to cut shapes from outlines that you have made. The older child can trace shapes from forms you have cut into plastic coffee can lids. You can do this easily with a sharp knife. *Caution:* Remember that it is the cutting experience that you are providing for, not a test for staying on lines.

Result: The child learns the technique of pasting and gluing paper and cardboard. He experiments with the use of space and becomes more aware of spatial limitations and organization. He is made to transfer concepts learned through body movement to a two-dimensional plane. He experiences the necessity of selecting from pieces differing in their material, shape, size, and color. This leads to a growing capability to make aesthetic judgments and to a sharpened sense of design and balance. He develops cutting and tearing skills and increases his understanding of the nature of the various types of paper used. His eye-hand coordination and visual-motor perception will improve as he reaches to select the items he wants to use. Using several kinds of materials in one project develops the child's sense of autonomy as he expands his knowledge of the physical world. He also develops an understanding of the concepts behind such terms as *big, little, thick, close together, on top of, next to, underneath, far apart, too big, too long, too wide,* and so forth. With some experience, you should be able to develop a wide variety of additional collage projects that will give the child much practice in seriation and in the classification of colors, textures, sizes, and shapes.

Transparent Materials

Provide pieces of white paper or cardboard that are at least 12″ × 18″. Provide containers of liquid starch and soft-bristled paint brushes or watercolor brushes. Provide a selection of colored tis-

David (4) applies scraps of cloth and tissue paper with liquid starch.

sue paper that has been cut into easy-to-handle sizes—small enough for the child to use directly or to cut into smaller pieces if he desires. Along with the tissue paper, you may supply small scraps of transparent cloth of interesting textures, such as organdy, chiffon, dotted swiss, and organza. The cloth must be lightweight in order to adhere to the paper with starch.

The child brushes the starch on either the background paper or on the piece of tissue paper or cloth to be fastened down. Then he arranges the scraps as a collage. This activity increases the child's awareness of textural differences and the arrangement of space. He also learns that tissue paper is transparent when wet, and he discovers the effect produced by overlapping transparent materials.

Children five years old and over may be interested in using specific colors for making trees, flowers, people, or other semi-representational figures in their collages. They can also use fine threads, yarns, and other lightweight items.

3-D Collages (Assemblages)

After some experiences with two-dimensional designs, you will want to introduce other materials into the collage activities. Solid items such as small seashells, pieces of wood, or any of the numerous items listed at the end of this book, add an exciting new dimension to collage making.

Provide individual squeeze bottles of white glue. Provide cardboard, paper plates, Mason jar lids, or some other solid material for the background. Place the collage materials on a lazy Susan, sometimes in individual containers and sometimes mixed together. Background sizes may vary from 2 inches to 2 feet. Use your imagination, but keep in mind the size of the materials being glued on.

The child puts the glue on either the background or the object to be fastened down. He presses the object against the background and holds it a few seconds to ensure that it sticks. The first time, suggest one or two objects for the child to start with. Then let him select what he wants to finish his project.

Variations
- Make a nature collage using items found on a nature walk.
- Make a seed collage, mixed with leaves or with grains, such as rice or barley.
- Make a bean collage with lima beans, navy beans, black-eyed peas.

- Use wooden pieces, including toothpicks, tongue depressors, ice-cream sticks, wooden spoons, bark, wooden wheels, spools.
- Use cloth only. Provide widely varying textures and densities. Add trimmings.
- Use dry breakfast foods only, such as Cheerios and Kix.
- Use wires that can be manipulated, such as pipe cleaners.
- Use white things only, such as popcorn, cotton, lace, buttons, egg shells, rice or tapioca.
- Use pastas, such as macaroni, noodles, spaghetti, rigatoni.
- Use soft things only, such as feathers, velvet, cotton, felt, fur.
- Use round, flat things only, such as washers, toy wheels, bottle caps.
- Use round things only, such as beads, spools, and marbles.
- Make your own variations, depending on the materials available and the concepts you want to teach. Frequently present mixed media.

Result: This experience increases the child's awareness of texture, shape, size, and other aspects of the physical world, such as gravity. It also serves as a visual-perceptual exercise as the child reaches and searches for additional items to use in his collage. He will have many opportunities to classify, categorize, and organize according to the challenges provided by the materials you have furnished. (*Note:* In areas serving very low-income groups, it is advisable to omit projects in which foods, such as cereals, beans, and macaroni, are used for decorative purposes. I would suggest using instead the nature and "found" items listed at the end of this book.)

The Older Child

The older child may wish to coordinate collage techniques with his pictorial representations. For example, he may first make a drawing of a thing or an event. He can then add to it various items from the collage collection. He may want to paste on buttons or beads for eyes, yarn or ribbon for hair, or fake fur for the skin of an animal.

You can introduce the child to mood collages, too. Try suggesting that he use the collage materials to make a picture of how he feels on a hot, sunny day. Or you might suggest he make a design about feeling happy, or tired, or hungry. After he has decided on a topic, guide him gently by making one or two suggestions of what he might use to start the picture. Be careful to suggest only. Keep in mind that your purpose is to give him a taking off point from which he can learn to do his own planning.

Result: The child learns to recognize that the thoughts of others, though similar to his, are individual. He learns that it is all right to express feelings and he is encouraged to recognize the existence of his own moods. He has practice in combining more than one art medium in a single picture, a technique that always adds interest and excitement to what may otherwise appear to be ordinary.

Cardboard Box Construction

After some experience with both two-dimensional and three-dimensional collages, the child can further his understanding of fastening one thing to another through the experience of cardboard box construction.

Jill, Roger, Samara, Nickie, Marc, and Manuel (all 3) are gluing wooden scraps together. When they are finished, they will paint them with tempera. Compare these assemblages with the constructions shown on page 151.

These containers were glued together and then painted. Ingenuity and individuality are evident in each one.

Provide all kinds of boxes collected over a period of time. Sizes should be varied, ranging from tiny jewelery boxes and toothpaste boxes, to soap, cereal, and shoe boxes. The round boxes that oatmeal, cleansers, and salt come in offer interesting challenges. Cardboard tubes from rolls of various household papers may be added, as well as some boxes without lids.

Two general approaches are used for these constructions. In the first, the child builds his construction by gluing together a selection of boxes. He may also be given a variety of tapes, strings, wire, and other materials to help in the more difficult fastening tasks. Smaller objects or items that offer contrasting textures may be added from the collage supply. The completed construction is then painted. The second approach is to paint the boxes before they are fastened together. The child then selects from an assortment of painted boxes the ones he wants to use for his particular construction. In painting these boxes, it is sometimes a good idea to scrub them first with a kitchen cleanser to provide a surface to which the paint will adhere more readily. Then add either milk or detergent to the paint to increase its covering and adhering power. Another ingredient to use with paint for this type of project is wheat paste. The wheat paste will help the paint to stick to very waxy surfaces.

Result: The child furthers his understanding of shapes and forms. He learns about balance and gravity and weight and counterbalance. In painting these constructions, he finds out about small corners, underneath, inside, all around, and comparative sizes. Because the paint adheres better to some surfaces than to others, he finds out about "waxy" and "too waxy." He learns to estimate time as he experiments with how long he has to hold one box against another to allow the glue to set enough to hold up on its own. He learns to improvise as he reinforces the glue with some of the other fastening materials provided. His self-esteem increases as he views his finished product.

SCISSORS

Benjie was excited when he saw the scissors.
Especially when the teacher said he could pick them
up and cut the paper she had given him. At home,
his mother never let him use her scissors. He took
the scissors in one hand and tried to cut the piece of
paper he had in his other. But nothing happened. The
paper kept sliding out between the scissors–still in
one piece. The teacher said, "I'll help you get started."
She showed him how to hold his hand with the
scissors in one place and to move the paper where he
wanted to cut it. Meanwhile, she sang this song:
> *O-pen, shut them, o-pen, shut them,*
> *O-pen and then shut.*
> *Move the pa-per round and rou-nd,*
> *That's the way to cut.*

Learning to use scissors is one of the important ego-building achievements of early childhood. The child discovers that scissors give him instant power to make changes in paper and other materials. Though other cutting tools may be forbidden, here is one that the child can use with full approval.

Cutting *looks* easy. The child readily understands the principle of opening and closing the scissors, and he will frequently spend long periods of time trying to master the technique. Tiny, immature finger muscles are not so easily directed to move in the manner necessary to guide and control the opening and closing. As previously stated, the ability to control the arm muscles develops from the shoulder downward. It reaches the extremities *only* after the other parts of the arm and hand have been developed. While these muscles are growing in maturity, the child uses and strengthens them, and gradually increases his skills.

Provide the best 5″, blunt-nosed scissors your budget will allow. If possible, obtain those with rubber-covered handles. These are of good quality and are available in both right- and left-handed scissors. Some 5″ clip-point scissors may also be supplied for older children.

If the child is left-handed, provide him with special "lefty" scissors. Once he has mastered the skill and has had practice in nursery school or kindergarten in cutting with these special scissors, he will be ready to learn to use the regulation scissors, which will be the type most usually available to him throughout his life.

For the child's first cutting efforts, be sure to provide paper that can be cut easily. If the paper is too thin, he will have difficulty manipulating it and the scissors may slip. If the paper is too thick he may find it difficult to exert sufficient pressure with his immature finger muscles. Poster paper, fadeless art paper, and butcher paper are good, easy-to-cut kinds of paper for beginners. Construction paper scraps can be used after the child is experienced with the lighter weights.

To understand the easiest way to use scissors, pick up your own scissors and notice the way *you* use them. Do you hold the paper still and move your hand around the cutting pattern? If so, your motions are like those of the young child who is learning to cut with scissors. The easy way is to hold the cutting hand as still as possible and move the *paper*. If you want to cut out a circle, the best way to do it is to manipulate the scissors while you move the paper around so that the scissors follow a circular path.

If the child is having much difficulty in handling scissors, helping him to learn this method can be useful. Don't worry about where the scraps fall at the beginning. Let him concentrate on cutting. It's a big task for a beginner. Be honest. Tell him it's hard.

Provide many opportunities for the child to cut paper freely, just for practice. Bring out stacks of scrap paper and ask the child to cut it into smaller pieces for you. Have scissors available whenever the child is working on paper collage.

Provide pictures from magazines. Ask the child to cut them out for you. At first, he may cut the picture right in half. But gradually, he will acquire the principle of cutting around the general shape of an object. Collections of old greeting cards are also fun to cut up, and, for a change of pace, give the child scraps of very thin Styrofoam, drinking straws, and broom straws.

Cutting on Lines

Being able to cut along a line requires the ability to control the individual parts of *both* hands while coordinating the movements visually. I don't feel that cutting on lines is important for a beginner, but recognizing shapes is. If the child learns to cut around the general shape formed by lines drawn on paper, he has acquired

Tracey (3½) and Larry (4) are cutting out circles they traced from a plastic coffee can cover.

one of the important skills that should be developed at the pre-school level.

Between 4 and 4½ years of age, most children have matured sufficiently to be able to cut along lines without experiencing frustration and failure. The child of six years who is unable to do so, may also have difficulty in reading or writing, or both. He should be given a perceptual-motor and visual screening to find the extent of his problem.

Pointed Scissors

The child of kindergarten age may be ready to use pointed scissors. But before he is given pointed scissors he must know how to handle them safely. Scissors are always handed to someone handle first. They are used only for cutting the material provided, and not for cutting hair, clothing, or other children. They are not to be held in the hand while the child walks around the room. A pair of 5″ scissors is good for general use.

During the period the child is learning to cut, he should also be given many opportunities to tear paper, especially large pieces. Start with tissue paper and newspaper until he masters the technique. Tearing paper will give him the satisfaction that he may not be able to get from cutting until he is able to fully control scissors. Tearing is not an easy activity because it calls for the use of the muscles that control the fingertips, which may not yet be fully developed.

Paper tearing also provides satisfying emotional experiences, relieves aggressive feelings, heightens the child's understanding of the material, and increases his awareness of shapes, sizes, and proportions. It also develops visual-motor perception, increases his ability to control his finger muscles, builds mechanical skills, imparts a fine sense of accomplishment, enlarges the child's means for creative expression, and increases his ability to judge sizes and shapes.

Montage

An excellent activity in which the child utilizes his cutting, pasting, and collage-making skills is creating a montage. A montage is made by superimposing many pictures and parts of pictures on one background to create an overall pictorial design. Provide the child with magazines that have many illustrations in them. At first, allow him to cut at random those pictures which appeal to him. To help the inexperienced child, you might first tear the pages out of the magazines so that he can make his selections and do his cutting from the loose pages, which are easier to handle. Provide a fairly stiff paper or cardboard background on which to arrange and paste the cut-out pictures. Usually a montage covers the entire paper, with one picture or part of a picture overlapping another so that the background doesn't show. Liquid paste is good for this project.

Montage projects are especially good to use in encouraging children to become further aware of their moods and feelings, an essential goal of creative developmental art. One day, for example, we decided to make a "quiet" montage. We looked through the pages of magazines and picked out a few quiet pictures. Some of the students brought quiet pictures from home: Pumpkin pie, a man's pipe, a mountain top, a bed, a sad monkey, a set of books. Each child cut out his own picture at his own particular

The teacher discusses *happy* feelings with Kira and Georgia (both 5) and Jill and Lori (both 5½) in preparation for making a Mood Collage.

level of ability. An 18″ × 24″ sheet of blue poster board was provided as a background. Each child chose the spot on the poster board that he wanted for his picture and pasted it on. We decided to leave a few empty spaces because, as one little girl observed, "The paper is quiet." The montage went up on the bulletin board for all to see. Sometimes it visited different classrooms to help other children learn to think about "quiet." It is brought out from time to time when quiet thoughts are needed. Sometimes it is covered over with a sheet of transparent blue plastic. Then it's *really* quiet.

On another occasion we made a "smile" montage. We cut out pictures of faces and faces and faces, all with smiles. These were pasted solidly next to each other, many of them overlapping, all around a small mirror. When we look at it, it reminds us to smile. We also made a "clothing" montage to help us learn the difference between winter and summer clothing. Some other good subjects for montage include clouds, people, animals, trees, flowers, and houses. Usually the montages are done as a class project, with three or four children at a time working on one picture.

The child may be interested in making his own individual montage, too. If so, provide him with a small enough sheet of background paper so that he can complete his design without tiring of it before he has finished.

Result: The child usually selects pictures purely by subject matter, showing little preference for either color or black and white. For the four- and five-year-old, this is a step toward mature cognitive growth where logic, rather than color or shape, will be the deciding factor of interpretation. Montage projects give the child experience in classifying, sorting, and arranging. He finds out that art is not only arrangement—it can also be the re-arrangement of someone else's pictures. He finds out about cooperative planning, and best of all, he finds out that he can make a real contribution to the classroom learning environment. Because the teacher takes care of his montages, uses them, and even lends them to other teachers, he knows that his efforts are appreciated, that he can be useful, and that he is an important member of the school community.

The finished *Happy* Mood Collages. (Top: Kira and Georgia; bottom: Jill and Lori.)

MANIPULATIVE
MATERIALS

Poke it and punch it. Then roll it round and round. Twist. Squeeze. Squeeze it hard. Squash it, flatten it out. Pile it up. Little tiny pieces, one giant shape. Young fingers and growing sensitivities explore the very essence of shape. Form. How to mold a world. How to build the future.

Clay

Clay is plastic and pliable, mobile and malleable. It is direct and responsive to the needs of young children and their emotions. When clay and child interact, there is a rhythmic flow of kinesthetic sensations that can provide escape for pent-up energies and satisfy the child's need to express his feelings. The soothing effect of this tactile medium as it is manipulated by the child can help to unburden anxieties and fears. As tensions are relaxed, the experience becomes one of intense sociability; it becomes the time for conversation and the expression of thoughts. Thus clay manipulation is an important developmental activity in many ways. There are several kinds of clay. Use all of them, but not at the same time.

Plasticine

One of the best kinds of clay for beginners is plasticine. Because it contains oil instead of water, plasticine remains pliable and can be used over and over again. It is smooth and does not stick to the hands and fingers, unless it is very warm. It is readily accepted by the young child who may hesitate to use the messier pottery clay. The children stacking balls of clay in the photograph on the preceding page are all 2½ years old.

There are different kinds of plasticine. It comes in varying degrees of softness. Since plasticine can be used over and over, it is best in the long run to purchase more expensive brands. It is usually obtainable through art supply stores. Excellent plasticine, medium soft in consistency, may be obtained in two-pound bricks.

Many colors are available. If you want to keep more than one color on hand, select two that will blend well together, such as yellow and green or brown and orange. If you give the child more than one color at a time, be prepared to have the colors permanently mixed together. Buy only those brands whose colors do not come off on the hands.

Before giving the clay to the child, give him a clay board (Masonite squares make good boards) or place plastic table mats or oilcloth on the worktable. New plasticine should be rolled into balls about the size of a child's fist before it is used. It should also be rolled into balls before it is put away after each use.

Place a ball of clay at each child's place or leave the clay in a container in the center of the table and let each child help himself. It does not need to be stored in covered containers and can be kept on open shelves. It will become somewhat firm when not in use, but it is quickly softened by the warmth of the hands or by a few minutes in the sunshine.

The child should know that clay must be kept off of floors and other people, and that he may not put it in his mouth. Beyond that, let him do what he wants with it. Avoid the temptation of providing patterns and models. Let each child discover what to do with it for himself. *No tools are needed* other than hands and fingers. The child should not be encouraged to employ sticks and other pointed objects in modeling the clay. These detract from the developmental benefits of finger manipulation.

Moist Modeling Clay

You should also provide moist modeling clay for the child to use. This is the traditional pottery clay, and is available ready mixed. It is an evenly textured, moist material that can be fired.

Give the child plenty of time to accustom himself to the difference between this clay and plasticine. Moist modeling clay will stick to his hands and clothing, but it can be brushed off when dry. It dries quickly. It is less elastic than plasticine clays but it is more responsive to shaping. Because this kind of clay hardens between uses, many children may be alarmed the first time they see this happening. An explanation of how moist modeling clay differs from plasticine will help them accept the fact that they are dealing with a different sort of clay.

Moist clay will be difficult to use if it is allowed to become too dry. It may become moldy or even rancid if it is kept too long in a covered container while it is too wet. If you control

Chris, Steve, Steven, Patricia, Shari, and Nickolas (all 4) share the experience of working with red modeling clay (which is moister than the gray clay shown in the photograph on the first page of this chapter). Using plenty of water enhances the kinesthetic and tactile values of this experience.

the moisture properly, however, moist clay can be stored indefinitely.

If the clay is stored in plastic bags, use two of them so that if one bag gets torn the other will still keep the clay from drying out. I usually dip the bag itself in water and shake it out loosely. This provides just enough moisture to keep the clay pliable. After placing the clay in the bag, pat the bag closely all around. For further protection, place the whole thing in a zippered plastic pillow case. Bend the top and seal it tightly with a rubber band, Twistee, or clothespin. Store the clay in a cool place. Any covered box, cupboard, or other container will do. The best container, of course, is a crock especially made for this purpose. For class use, try galvanized garbage cans, which are available in small, easy-to-handle, sizes. Moisture can be controlled by putting one or more wet sponges into the storage container. Another method of controlling moisture is to poke a small hole in each ball of clay and fill it with water before storage. To test clay that has not been used for a while, roll a small piece in your hands. If it is very sticky, it is too wet; if it cracks quickly, it is too dry. If you want to store clay for brief periods only—during class time, for example—just cover it with wet rags or towels.

If the clay has become too wet, spread it out to dry. Brief exposure to the air will soon make it more usable. Spreading it on an absorbent surface, such as Celotex or cloth-covered boards, will speed the drying process. After the clay has dried sufficiently, knead it well to remove all air bubbles and to smooth it out.

If the clay has become too dry, break it up, smash it if necessary, and soak it in water for one or two days. After the clay has softened, pour off the surplus water, and then treat it as you would clay that has become too wet. Soon it can be made workable again. Don't worry about using very old clay. It will keep almost indefinitely.

Pottery clay is also available in powdered form at a great saving in cost. Directions for mixing are found on the containers. The experience of mixing the powder helps the child to understand and appreciate the composition of clay and its uses. It is always best to mix the clay about two days before it is to be used. Doing so helps the child develop an awareness of the concept of time, happily anticipating playing with clay when it is ready.

The color of most pottery clay, whether it is moist or powdered, is buff or gray. Both kinds are also obtainable in luscious, brownish-orange terra-cotta. When dry, it is the color of Mexican potteryware and is so strong that it does not have to be fired. The powder can be obtained in an easy-to-mix form in its own plastic bag. Just add water to the bag, knead the clay inside the bag, and it is ready to use. Be sure to give the child an opportunity to use red clays. The color increases his appreciation of clay.

Use red pottery clay the same way you use your other clays. Because it dries more rapidly than the other clays, provide water with which to pat and moisten the clay as the child uses it. Show the child how to dip his fingers into the water and moisten the clay with his wet fingertips. Some children enjoy wetting and patting the clay to the point where it disappears altogether. When that happens, give him another piece. The process is far more important than preserving the clay. Store red clay as you do buff modeling clay, but provide much more moisture, as it dries out more quickly.

In the beginning, use pottery clay the same way you use plasticine. Provide each child with his own ball of clay, the larger the better. Have additional clay within easy reach in case he feels that he needs more. Instead of giving each child an individual clay board, I like to spread an oilcloth on the table when pottery clay is being used. This gives the child more space for freedom of movement. Another way to present clay is to put all of it in one large free-form mass on the table for a group of children to work on together. Usually the child needs no encouragement to know what to do. He will poke, pound, pull, and pat. He will add more clay to his original piece. Then he will pull it apart. He may form very small individual shapes, or he may pile one big lump on top of another. However he handles it, whatever he makes, he experiences the joy of responding to his need for creative expression. Again, avoid patterns and models. At the conclusion of the activity, roll the clay into balls for storage.

Eventually the child will try to make figures of people or animals. He will usually become frustrated when he tries to fasten on arms and legs, a difficult task. Show him how he can "pinch out" the shape to form the arms and legs. Making pinch figures is very easy for the young child, and it provides an excellent means for further development of the small muscles that control the fingers. If you demonstrate this technique for the child, don't put too much emphasis on it and don't leave your own pinch figures intact, so the child doesn't feel they are models for him to follow.

If you want to allow the pottery clay pieces to harden permanently, but do not have access to a kiln, add dextrin (obtainable from any drug store) to the clay before modeling. Dextrin is made from corn and comes in white and yellow. Use only the yellow. The following mixtures will give sufficient hardening quality for your use: 1 part dextrin to 19 or 20 parts powdered clay; or 1 teaspoon dextrin to 1 pound moist clay. If you add it to powdered clay, do so before you mix the powder with water. When using dextrin with moist clay, knead it into the clay thoroughly. Because of its strong and quick hardening quality, do not mix more than you plan to use immediately.

Pot Making

Although we generally recommend that you avoid the use of models and patterns, this does not mean that you should avoid all demonstrations of how to handle craft materials. Pottery clay is an excellent medium for the introduction of beginning craft work.

One of the easiest objects for a child to make is the Push Bowl. It is made by rolling a small piece of clay into a ball, and then simply punching a hole in it with thumb or fingers. Simple for the young child as any craft can be, yet it contains all the elements of creative productivity. Introduce it only after the child has had many months of free-form expression. Again, it is not necessary to provide a pattern for the child. Motivate him by making three or four bowls yourself, while he watches. Talk to him about what you are doing. After each bowl is made, roll up the clay and start another. Also make some free-form bowls, but roll them up each time so that the child will not have a model to copy. After your demonstration, suggest to the child that he take some clay and find out for himself how easy it is to make a bowl. Tell him he may make a Push Bowl like you did or he may invent his own method. As he gains a little experience, encourage him to improvise. His bowl may or may not look like a bowl to you, but it will not be merely a copy.

Result: Working with clay is one of the most beneficial creative activities for a child. The manipulation of the clay will greatly improve his control of the small muscles of his hands and fingers. The flexibility, plasticity, adaptability, unpredictability, and messiness of clay all present problem-solving challenges that will improve the child's ability to cope with the physical world. He will increase his awareness of three-dimensional shape and design and of the effects of gravity. He will learn to be responsible for the care of materials and will have good practice in sharing materials and ideas. He will take pride in his clay pieces as he creates new shapes. He will release his tensions as he pats, pounds, pulls, and tears apart pieces of clay.

Painting Clay

Red, gray, or buff pottery clay may be painted with tempera when dry. Provide several bright, clear colors for the child to choose from. Use good-quality watercolor brushes that have fine points. The child may use white, too, which is very attractive on clay pieces. I usually offer the child the white paint *after* he has finished with the other colors. It adds an attractive accent.

Wedging

Each time you re-use a piece of clay, be sure to wedge it to remove *all* air bubbles. Clay is wedged by slamming and slapping it over and over against a hard tabletop or clay board. The child will take great delight in helping to do this.

If clay is to be fired, remember that it will dry more slowly on the inside than on the outside. Keep the object covered with wet rags to keep the outside moist until the inside has had some chance to dry. Dry clay shrinks somewhat. Therefore, if the outer layer dries faster than the inside, the object will crack.

If a clay object that is to be fired is larger than your fist, it is a good idea to hollow it out somewhat from the underside to allow for more even drying. Thin pieces and small pieces dry more evenly than thick or large pieces. However, if it is too thin, it will break.

Self-hardening commercial clays that do not need to be fired are also available. They are quite expensive, but good for experimental use on small projects.

Play Dough

The play dough and other homemade materials of similar nature that I want to tell you about should not be used in place of clay. They can be used, however, as an extension and reinforcement of that manipulative material. You may provide rolling pins, cookie cutters, modeling tools, and other such accessories for the child to use with these materials if you wish.

Flour, salt, and water are the basic ingredients of play dough. For general use, to make cookies, pies, and other make-believe foods, mix:

> 3 parts flour
> 1 part salt
> 1 part water

Knead the ingredients until they take on the proper consistency. If you vary the proportions, the amount of water you use should be equal to the amount of salt. Play dough can be kept in good condition for about two weeks if it is kept in an airtight container. By adding 1 teaspoon of alum for each 2 cups of flour, you can keep the mixture for several months.

Variations
- Add food coloring to the water to color the dough.
- Add salad oil (1 tablespoon to 1 cup of flour) to make the mixture more elastic.
- For modeling small objects, to harden and later paint, make

Salt Dough, using more salt and less water. When a larger
amount of salt is used, the alum is less important because salt
also acts as a preservative.

- For the very young child, make soft, pliable Cloud Dough:

1 cup salad oil
6 cups flour
1 cup water

Use just enough water to bind the mixture. Start with the quantity called for in the recipe and then add 1 tablespoonful at
a time if more is needed. Knead the mixture. Cloud Dough
will be very oily, but it supplies an unusual tactile experience.

- Cornstarch Dough is another interesting kind of dough:

1 part cornstarch
3 parts salt
1 part water

Heat the water and salt for a few minutes, then slowly add
the cornstarch, stirring until well mixed. Knead the dough and
add more water if necessary. This dough will dry without crack-
ing.

- You may also want to try Oatmeal Dough:

1 part flour
2 parts oatmeal
1 part water

Add the water gradually to bind the mixture. Cornmeal can
be used to vary the texture. Coffee grounds, in small quantities,
also add textural interest, but too many grounds will prevent
hardening.

Papier-Mâché Pulp

Papier-mâché activities should be reserved for children who are
at least five years old. Have some children help you tear three
double sheets of newspaper into small pieces. Unfold the paper
before tearing it. Completely cover the torn paper with boiling
water. Let it stand in the water a few minutes, then stir the mixture
until it forms a pulp. Mix 6 tablespoons of wheat paste with 2
cups of water. Stir this mixture into the wet pulp. When it is
cool enough, knead the pulp with your hands until it is well-mixed
and sticky. This mixture can be used to shape small objects. When
they dry, the child can sand them smooth and paint them. It
is best to mix the pulp just before use. It does not keep for more

than a couple of days, and then only if it is stored in a completely airtight container. There are also many commercial preparations, such as Shreddimix, that can be used instead of homemade papier-mâché.

Dough-making Activities

The finest experience that can be given a child with play dough is to let him make his own. Almost any combination of the basic ingredients will result in a satisfactory dough. The child may never get around to making anything with his "dough," but he will have grown in his overall learning by having mixed it. As in paint mixing, provide small quantities of ingredients for the child to mix. The children should work in groups of two or three. This activity requires the following items: a bowl of flour and a scoop, a smaller bowl and a smaller scoop for salt (or, if you prefer, a box of salt from which to pour), a small pitcher of water, and a dispenser bottle with a very small opening for salad oil (liquid sweetener or hand lotion bottles are satisfactory).

Give each child a small container in which to mix the ingredients. Disposable aluminum foil baking pans or bowls, or large plastic cereal dishes are fine. Provide tablespoons for mixing with. The child will soon discard them in favor of fingers and hands. Provide an extra amount of trust. If the child seems to be "stuck," suggest he experiment to find out if he needs additional quantities of one or more of the ingredients. He may try oil, water, or salt before discovering for himself that the mixture needs more flour. Tell the child that when the mixture does not stick to his hands, it is ready to use.

When allowing children to perform self-directed experiments such as making their own play dough or paint, it is usually best to restrict the number of children working in any one area at a time to two or three. This number working together have the maximum amount of freedom and self-supervision. They are able to share with one another, give each other assistance, and make suggestions, while still concentrating on their own individual experiments. If there are more than three, the experience is apt to become teacher-dominated with too many directions. It is always easier to supervise small groups with each individual working on his own experiment, than to watch over one large group in which everyone is supposed to be doing the same thing. With one large group too much of your attention may be diverted to the child who is deviating or to the one who is setting the

Jeri (4) and Rael (3½) carefully combine the ingredients for play dough. The quantities of the ingredients placed on the table are controlled so that each child can only experience success, although he may have to experiment with various combinations to achieve the proper consistency.

best example. The children between these two extremes may be ignored; you will have difficulty in recognizing and meeting their individual needs. This holds true for almost any type of classroom activity.

Extend the child's interest in this important activity by adding small amounts of food coloring or powdered tempera to the dough. Since making play dough is a somewhat complicated procedure for the child, it is best to save the addition of color until after the dough is made. The color can even be added the next day. Then the child can be given food coloring with plastic droppers with which he can color his dough. Or he can sprinkle powdered tempera onto his mixture. Either way, he then kneads it until it is blended. Most children will make their dough quite oily, and the colors will blend in easily. If the mixture is fairly dry, however, it will not take the color as well. (*Note:* When you are mixing dough yourself for the child to play with, you can add the powdered tempera directly to the flour before mixing. This is not a good method for the child to use because it does not enable him to experience the finger manipulation involved in adding the color *after* the dough is mixed.)

Result: The child increases his knowledge of proportion, quantity, measurement. He develops a conceptual awareness of the difference in measuring dry ingredients and liquids. He increases his awareness of textural differences and sensitivity to touch, and his awareness of the concepts behind the terms *oily, floury, sticky, mushy, thick, thin,* and other descriptive words. He experiences the emotional well-being that accompanies satisfying sensory explorations. He also displays an awareness of his own creativity and inventiveness as he shows a strong possessiveness for his *own* dough. When he adds color to the completed play dough, he has an additional opportunity to exercise and develop the small muscles of his fingers and hands. Some children have much difficulty in manipulating their fingers so as to mix in the color. The observant teacher can use this as a clue to which child may need more experiences in the use of his fine muscles.

WOODWORKING

Driving past a new construction project with my two-year-old grandson, I slowed the car down so that he could see the wonderful things that were going on. But he began to cry: "Poor house. All broken. Man break house. Bad man." He saw wood being cut. He saw things being hit with hammers. He saw people doing all kinds of no-no's. Two years later, he was the proud owner of a man-sized tool chest, complete with small, but very real tools of all kinds. A saw. Hammer. Hand drill. Level. Screwdriver. Vise. A tape measure and a T-square. And he knew how to use them. He knew about sandpaper. He knew how to saw a piece of soft wood, glue it, hammer it, or even, sometimes, tape it. He decorated his pieces with all kinds of intriguing items he had picked up around his home: a broken comb, a peanut shell, a piece of tile, a cardboard box. He had a wooden box, around the four edges of which slots for sawing had been started for him. This enabled him to work independently, without someone having to manipulate the vise for him or nail the piece he wanted to saw to a heavy block of wood. But whether he was sawing, gluing, decorating, or putting everything away, always one thing was overwhelmingly in evidence: pride. Pride of accomplishment that comes with the proper handling of real tools; of building, not tearing down; of creating, not manufacturing.

Woodworking is another experience that will enable the child to explore the physical aspects of his environment and give him an opportunity to create something new of his very own. First he makes a choice, selecting the material he wishes to use. Perhaps he knows in advance what he wants to do with it, or perhaps he just wants to "work," exploring the role of an adult. The child likes to saw and hammer. The physical activity, the concentration, the release of emotional energy and aggressive feelings—all these things make him feel good. Wood is a living material and the child likes the feel of it. He likes to touch it and even to smell it. With a little guidance, he can learn to take a simple block of wood, sand it smooth, wax it, and buff it. And he can learn about fine craftsmanship.

The Wood Supply

White pine, spruce, and poplar are soft woods that the child can saw and hammer easily. The wood should be smooth and free of splinters and knots. Boards should be cut with the grain running lengthwise. To check on this, lay the board on a flat surface and look at the narrow edge. The grain should run horizontally rather than vertically or at an angle.

Balsa wood is very soft and easy to use, but it is quite expensive. Pine moldings and dowels can also be used. Supply wooden crates for the child to use in practicing sawing. Make ¼" slots every two inches around the top edges of the crate. The child can use these slots to saw with a minimum amount of supervision. Out of doors, the child can saw on and pound nails into tree stumps and logs.

Also get all kinds of wood scraps, shavings from a cabinet shop, spools, knobs, wooden buttons, and similar items. The child can also make use of twigs, branches, roots, and other kinds of wood found outdoors.

Scraps that are not cut with the grain and scraps that have knots in them should not be used for sawing, but may be used for gluing activities. Plywood scraps, which are difficult to saw and hammer, are also good for glued constructions. Wood gluing constructions are, in fact, an excellent tie-in between block building and carpentry.

Your wood collection may be supplemented with wallboard, pegboard, cork, floor tile, and other scrap building materials. Styrofoam blocks can be used for the very young child when he is first learning to saw.

The Work Area

When carpentry tools are used, a work area should be set up away from the flow of classroom traffic and away from other children who are playing. Workbenches should be about 15" from the floor, and they must be sturdy. A suitable workbench can be made from two child-size sawhorses (or from two adult-size sawhorses that have had the legs cut down). Place the sawhorses about 3 or 4 feet apart. Then nail a heavy board, at least two inches thick, to the two sawhorses. One child can hammer and saw at each end of the board, and use the space between the sawhorses for tools and supplies. Actually, any heavy table that is an appropriate height can serve as a workbench.

Tools

Vise. A child cannot usually get good leverage while he is sawing. Therefore, a vise should be used to hold the wood in place in case the saw slips. If a vise is not available, nail the wood to the workbench to hold it securely in one place while the child is working on it. Use two nails to prevent a pivoting effect.

Hammer and Saw. The two basic tools for working with wood are a hammer and a saw. Toy ones are unsatisfactory. Therefore, provide the child with small-sized, real tools. Before buying a hammer, make sure that the head is securely wedged in place. You should also provide the child with a claw hammer for pulling out nails. This can be a regular-sized tool. Cross-cut saws that are short in length and have sturdy handles are the most desirable kind of saw for the young child.

Drill. A drill for boring holes in wood is another valuable woodworking tool. A hand drill that works like an old-fashioned egg-

Dani (5½) at the workbench. The board he is sawing is nailed to the bench with two nails.

Dani's picture of himself at the workbench. The elaborate headdress is an indication of the feelings of importance and satisfaction that resulted from the woodworking experience—feelings that were enhanced by the fact that he was photographed while doing it.

beater is easier to manipulate than a brace and bit. Toy electric drills are available, and they work well on soft wood.

Other Tools.   The child should also be introduced to other tools at this time, including pliers and screwdrivers. These should be real tools, sturdy and of good weight, but not very large. A 4″ screwdriver is appropriate. Metal squares and rulers are also important learning tools. A rasp is dangerous for the young child, and it should be used only under very close supervision. Levels are also educational and easy to use. A toy level, if it really works, is satisfactory. A wide variety of screws and nails should also be provided. Nails with large heads are preferable, but the child should also have the opportunity to work with 6-penny and 8-penny nails. Avoid roofing nails, for they can be quite dangerous if they are stepped on. Screws that are narrow and have flat heads are easier for the child to handle than those with rounded tops.

Storing Tools

If space allows, provide a pegboard rack on which to hang the tools. Under each hook attach a small drawing of the tool that belongs on it. I prefer this method to the common one of outlining the whole tool. The small drawing will give the child a better understanding of substitute symbols. The drawings may also have the name of the tool printed above it to further the concept of symbolization.

The child can also be taught to use a tool box, which may be necessary where there is limited storage space. He must learn to return the tools to their proper place.

Another storage method is to use a separate container for each type of tool. Each container can be labeled with a drawing and the name of the tool that belongs in it.

Rules for Woodworking Activities

For the child's safety, certain rules must be followed when he is working with tools. He should understand what the rules are and know why he must obey them. The rules include the following:

- Tools must always be handled properly and with care.
- Tools are never laid down on the workbench when the child is finished with the activity. They must always be replaced in the tool box or hung on the appropriate hook.
- Tools must never be taken away from the immediate working area.
- One child must never hold a board in place for another.

150   If you have a child in your group who is not ready to follow the strict rules that are necessary for woodworking activities, it is possible to give him similar experiences that are in the realm of his readiness. For example, you can let him saw on the sides of boxes, using a pre-cut slot for a starting point. Let him saw on logs or tree stumps out of doors. Give him very soft wood and a lightweight hammer for pounding nails. Give him scraps of wood with small holes drilled in them to pound nails into. Let him hammer nails into pieces of wall board or Styrofoam.

Woodworking Activities

The child will find many things to do with wood and tools. He can saw pieces of wood or the edges of wooden boxes. He can hammer nails. He can drill holes. He can use sandpaper to smooth surfaces, edges, and corners. He can help repair wooden playground equipment. He can make abstract objects or representational objects. He can attach wheels that turn to pieces of wood. He can make stabiles. He can glue wood scraps together to create fascinating figures.

When the child has completed a woodworking project, he may wish to decorate it with a permanent finish. He may cover it with any of the following: powdered tempera paint mixed with milk instead of water, powdered tempera paint with wheat paste, water-based acrylic paint, enamel over a good undercoater, clear shellac or varnish, clear plastic finishes, or crayons.

Result: The child derives a great deal of satisfaction and develops a sense of power and self-esteem as he accomplishes "adult" tasks with adult equipment. He learns carpentry skills in accordance with his level of ability and he learns the importance of handling tools with care. He develops an awareness of his relationship to others as he learns to handle the tools in a way that will not cause danger to other children. He also learns to keep a sufficient amount of space between himself and other children when he works with tools. He grows in his ability to make a plan and carry it to a conclusion. He increases his mathematical concepts in relation to weight, thickness, shape, volume, length, and width. He releases emotional tensions and satisfies needs to express aggressive feelings in a legitimate manner. He develops a new concept of representational design as he begins to relate what he is making with the real thing. He sometimes follows up a satisfying carpentry experience with his first attempts at representational drawing.

Wood constructions. The two small ones in front and the large one on the right were made by 3½-year-olds. The large one in the center was made by a 4-year-old, and the large one on the left by a 5½-year-old. Both girls and boys enjoy this activity.

Whittling

The five-year-old child can be taught simple whittling procedures. Help him find a pungent bush or tree from which small twigs may be taken. Select twigs that have an unbroken length of from 10″ to 14″. With a paring knife, show him how to whittle gently in a direction away from his body. Teach him to support the hand in which he holds the twig by resting it against his body to keep it steady. Tell him to always keep his eye on the knife so that he knows exactly what it is doing at all times. Caution him to work slowly and gently. Motivate him to do so by your own relaxed and trusting attitude as you sit next to him. After he whittles the upper portion of his twig, give him some sandpaper to smooth it with.

Result: The child learns to handle a knife with extreme caution. He learns to perform a task according to a given method and takes pride in his ability to do so. He increases his eye-hand coordination and visual-motor perception. Bracing the twig against his body heightens the kinesthetic sensation and emotional satisfaction of this experience.

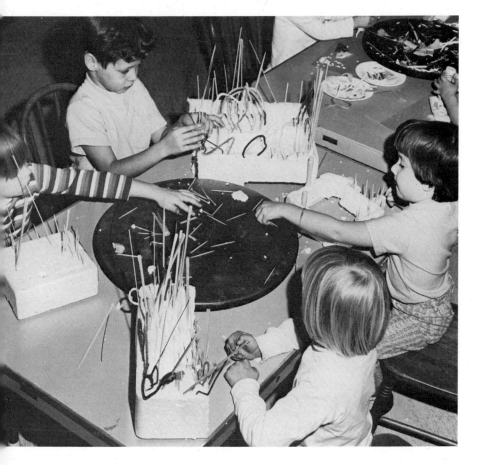

STYROFOAM

It was just a piece of Styrofoam, cut round to resemble the shape of a birthday cake. The teacher had glued it to a piece of heavy cardboard, also round, but larger, to hold the lightweight material in place while it was being worked on. Today was Anna's birthday and her friends helped her to decorate "the most beautiful cake in the world." It was festooned with green and pink pipe cleaners which sprouted abruptly in surprising but harmonious clumps about the top surface. Around the upper rim of the cake were dozens of pastel-colored toothpicks, around which had been woven in a delightful five-year-old un-pattern, strands of pink and green yarn and ribbons, the many loose ends casually hanging over the edges like scraggly bangs. Here and there various sizes of candles blossomed out of the surface, their tips decorated with bits and pieces of aluminum foil giving each candle the appearance of having several silver-flamed tops. A few sparkling jewels from the collage collection completed the creation. It was lovingly carried to the table where the birthday party, with cupcakes and bonbons, was about to begin.

Styrofoam and other brands of molded plastic foam are inexpensive, lightweight, easy to handle, interestingly textured, and have an easy-to-poke-into surface that lends itself well to the creative activities of young children. The ease with which it can be controlled makes it highly satisfying to the child. The ease with which it can be obtained makes it highly satisfying to the teacher who may need to worry about budgets and sources of materials.

Styrofoam may be purchased commercially in many different shapes and thicknesses. It can be obtained in sheets so thin that they can be cut with scissors. Larger pieces, up to four inches thick and one foot wide, are also available. These thicker pieces can be easily cut with an ordinary bread knife or a small saw. (*Hint:* When cutting Styrofoam, smooth the cut edges and sides by rubbing them with another piece of Styrofoam, as you would with sandpaper on wood.)

Commercial Styrofoam is generally obtainable in white. Blue is also fairly popular and green Styrofoam is frequently used by florists. Styrofoam paint is obtainable in spray cans, but we generally do not use it in nursery school or kindergarten.

Scrap Styrofoam and plastic foam are readily available. The best places to get them are electrical and electronic supply houses, since much of their equipment comes packed in it. These packing pieces, which may also be obtained from hardware stores, usually come in interesting shapes, since they have been formed to encase the merchandise with its exact shape.

People who decorate for banquets and parties also use Styrofoam, and they may be willing to give you their leftover scraps. Florist shops, too, frequently have such scraps.

Try to keep on hand large squares and rectangles, balls of various sizes, flat pieces in various shapes and thicknesses, pieces thin enough to cut with scissors, cones and dowels (which are especially available during the Christmas season), scraps cut from larger pieces, and packing shapes and forms.

Some items that are useful in decorating these various types of plastic foam and in making stabiles are:

Pipe cleaners	Beads	Wood scraps
Wire strips	Corks	Nails and screws
Wood dowels	Feathers	Ribbon, yarn, and
Thread	Toothpicks	other trimmings
Broom straws	Springs	Macaroni and spaghetti
Jewelry	Drinking straws	Spools
Chains	Clothespins	Ice Cream sticks
Twigs	Tongue depressors	Artificial flowers

Stabiles

Unlike mobiles, which are delicately balanced forms that hang and sway with the breeze, stabiles are fairly easy for the very young child to create without much adult assistance. Stabiles are similar to mobiles except that they do not hang and their parts may or may not move. Give the child a piece of Styrofoam or other plastic foam. You can make several sizes available. Also give him an assortment of things with which to decorate his stabile.

Many children have had a hand in decorating the Styrofoam motorcycle packing mold. Saundra (3½) is beautifying the upper left corner with hairpins. Bradley (4½) is trying to find a way to stick on some oversized drinking straws, which bend too easily. Seth (5½) is adding popsicle sticks, which are also difficult to stick into the tightly pressed foam.

Styrofoam assemblages are usually put together and taken apart many times during an activity session when they are in use. The small piece in front was assembled by a 2½-year-old. The other pieces (from left to right) were made by a 3-year-old, a 4-year-old, and a 5-year-old.

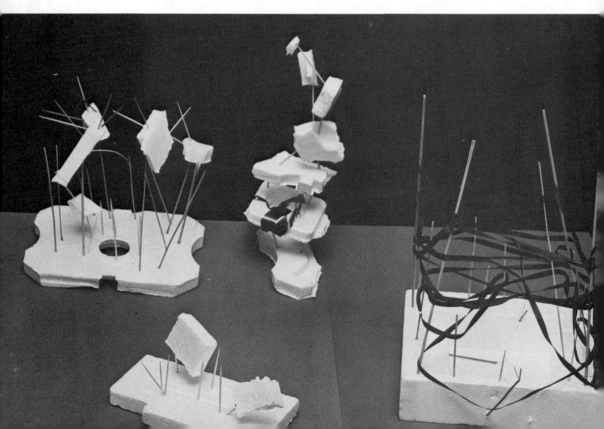

Usually he will stick on a few items and let his imagination take him from there. Let the child know that he may use the materials in any way he wishes to make his own design.

Variations
- Have two or three children work on one large project. Combine paint, three-dimensional materials, and imagination.
- Have the child glue together very small scraps of Styrofoam and then decorate his object with paint, scraps of cloth, and other appropriate items.
- Restrict the child to only a few selected materials, such as round Styrofoam balls and pipe cleaners.
- Have the child paint the plastic foam before he decorates it. Use tempera paint on Styrofoam, and watercolor on the smoother-finished plastic foams.

Result: The child will display amazing ingenuity in the way he combines the materials. He will experience problems of balance and weight as he decorates one side of the stabile too heavily and learns to solve this difficulty by counterbalancing. He will usually enter into this activity readily, even if, like some children, he is hesitant about painting or clay work. This serves as one way to orient a confused or hesitant child to creative experiences. He has an opportunity to practice many of the manipulative tricks he has learned from the various table games, puzzles, blocks, and similar materials that are part of his daily play. He also increases his aesthetic awareness as he works to make his piece *beautiful*.

PRINT MAKING

*It can be fingerpaint handprints all over a paper
tablecloth to decorate for an open house. It can be
circles in neat rows made from spray-can tops dipped
in paint. It can be squares, triangles, or free-form
shapes made from a wide variety of gadgets, parts
of games, or cut into pliable material such as
vegetables or erasers. However it's made, whatever
the material, it's learning about design.*

Printing is a simple method of transferring a design from the
surface of an object to some other surface, such as a piece of
cardboard or paper. The object is dipped in paint or ink and
then pressed or stamped on the surface to which the design is
to be transferred.

Print making introduces a new concept to the child—the reverse
image. Except for a few projects, such as Butterfly Blots and
Monoprints, the art experiences we have discussed so far all involve
fashioning or creating something directly. Now, with print-making
projects, the child will discover that the design he makes will be
reversed when he prints it.

The child can employ a wide variety of articles in making prints.
Here are some he can use directly without having to change them
in any way:

Wood blocks	Dominoes	Seashells
Wood scraps	Bottle caps	Kitchen utensils
Spools	Jar lids	Cookie cutters
Plastic toys	Erasers	Checkers
	Sponges	

In addition to these materials, you can cut original designs or
geometric shapes into an art gum or some other kind of soft
eraser. You can also cut a design into root vegetables, such as
carrots, potatoes, or parsnips. You can make small, individual
printing blocks for each child from plasticine. With a toothpick
or some other implement, the child can scratch an outline onto
the surface of one end of the block. Another interesting printing

device can be made by gluing pieces of felt, cork, cord, and other materials onto the surface of a small paint roller. Dip the roller lightly in paint or ink and roll it across a piece of paper to produce a design. Wads of wet paper make yet another kind of printing block. Simply wad a piece of wet paper into a ball, dip it in dry paint, and blot it onto another surface.

Paint and Ink

The best kind of paint to use for printing projects is liquid tempera. Paint or ink is ordinarily applied by pressing the printing block onto an ink pad or paint pad, or by dipping it into a shallow

Phyllis (4) prepares a paint pad to use in making white Valentine prints on red paper. Her tools include a heart-shaped kitchen sponge, a heart-shaped potato half, and the end of a carrot.

dish of paint. Cottage cheese carton lids make good containers for this purpose. Ink pads can be purchased ready made. An effective paint pad can be made by putting two layers of folded paper towels in a flat dish and pouring a small amount of tempera paint over them. Let the towels stand for a few minutes until they soak up the paint. Dab the printing object onto the paint pad lightly and then press it on a piece of paper to transfer the print. The older child may wish to apply the paint to the object with a brush rather than use a paint pad.

Paper and Colors

Any paper suitable for painting is suitable for printing. Novelty papers can be used effectively. Use light colors on dark paper, or dark colors on light paper for varying effects.

Variations
- Use several shades of one color on paper of the same color, but in lighter or darker shades. This will give an effect of really being *printed* on the paper by machines.

Finished prints. They can be used for gifts or decorations. Children of any age can make them.

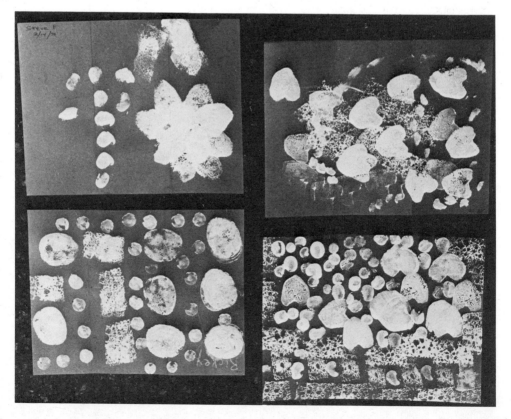

- Use seasonal colors for holiday projects.
- Have several objects for the same shape or design, and use a different color to print each one in order to create an interesting design.
- Print on tissue paper to make gift wrapping paper.
- Print on muslin squares with ink.
- Use cardboard rather than paper.
- Print the design with ink, then paint over it with transparent watercolor.
- Make a design using ink or paints, then finish the project with crayon or marking pens.

Result: The child acquires a concept of making prints. At about five years of age he may develop the concept of mirror image as a result of his printing activities. He has an opportunity to practice principles of design that he has been developing in his other art experiences. He enjoys the ease with which he is able to create a controlled design and he learns the advantage of planning for design. He is able to increase his awareness of space and size as he makes decisions regarding what fits into some particular space. He also becomes aware of the concept of overlapping which gives him an introduction to perspective.

SPECIAL ACTIVITIES

*To experiment and to discover for one's own self!
To investigate and try out and to proceed at one's
own pace! To make one's own selections of
materials and to look only within one's own mind
to decide on their use! The infinite nature of
imagination! The thrill of self-discovery! The
satisfaction of self-accomplishment! The growth of
an individual!*

Blocks and Boxes

Through the medium of creative art experiences, it is possible
to take various areas of the curriculum and slowly build them
into one many-faceted unit with multiple learning opportunities.
Such units are appropriate for the young child because they don't
confine him to an isolated topic in which he may not be interested,
but they offer many opportunities for taking off into individual
tangents and interests.

Several areas of study had been going on in our school over
a period of weeks. The introduction into the classroom of a new
cash register and its placement in the block cupboard led to a
vast ever-growing, ever-changing supermarket mushrooming
from the block-building corner out into the center of the classroom. Each new day and each new construction saw an ever-more
elaborate structure expanding into a complex of many rooms
and divisions.

In the hallway, just outside of the classroom, but still within
range of the teacher's supervision, a few children at a time were
allowed to play with some large refrigerator packing cartons that
had been given to the school. The boxes were large enough for
a child to walk into. They were used as tunnels, hideouts, trains,
wigwams, space ships, and many other intriguing, magical things.

During these same weeks, the teachers had been helping each
child learn his home telephone number. This had led to a study
of the telephone, practice in how to answer it, and much play
with both toy and real phones. One day the teacher made a bulletin

board display of telephone booths. As a result, the children decided they would like to make a "real" telephone booth. One child suggested using one of the packing cartons and the others agreed that it would be a good idea.

The floor was covered with newspaper and a box was brought in to be painted. The teacher provided red liquid tempera, red powdered tempera, two cans of condensed milk, and several containers to mix the paint in. When it was his turn to work on the telephone booth, each child mixed his own supply of paint. Using canned milk to thin out the paint gave it a hard, permanent, slightly glossy finish that when dry would not rub off. Two-, three-, and four-inch brushes were also provided. By painting this large box, the children became more aware of such concepts as *top, bottom, the other side,* and so forth. They also discovered that it takes a long time to paint a big cardboard box. They learned that the larger the brush used, the less time it takes to cover an area. They found that it took two coats of paint to cover the printing on the box and that the box looked better if the paint was applied with long, smooth strokes rather than with short dabs. They also discovered that splashed paint needs to be wiped up right away before it dries because the milk formed a hard finish.

After the box was painted, the teacher cut a door into one side of the box, and a window into the door. She fastened a plastic toy wall telephone to one wall of the box with 3″ bolts (heads on the outside). Each child wrote his name and phone number in a telephone book which hung in the booth. The children placed a hollow block inside the box for a seat.

The chief engineers of the supermarket project decided that the phone booth should be located in their "shopping center." When they saw that the phone booth towered far above their wooden blocks, the children decided they needed a new kind of supermarket. The blocks were stacked away and the remaining cartons were brought into the area. The children selected a bright lavender paint to use on the boxes. Condensed milk was added to the paint as before. The teacher first cut one side out of each of the boxes to make a doorway. Each child took his turn painting the boxes with the creamy milk and paint mixture. The lavender paint on the light-brown corrugated cardboard produced a fluorescent effect that the children found exhilarating. Most adults thought that the lavender clashed somewhat with the red of the telephone booth, but the children thought the color combination was quite beautiful.

This activity reinforced what the children had learned when

Leo, Kira, and John

Jill and Stevie

James, Terri, Anne, Roger, Michael, and Stephen

Stephen

The cardboard city.

Blocks, boxes, and box sculpture
for 5-year-olds.

they painted the telephone booth, and it taught them some new things. They discovered that the corners of a very big box were just as small as the corners of a little box—and just as hard to get paint into. They discovered that it takes much longer to paint both the inside and outside of a box than it does to paint only the outside. They observed that the lavender paint didn't dry to as glossy a finish as the red paint had, probably because the lavender had some white in it.

Notes were sent home to the children's families asking them to save their empty food containers for the class to use in stocking the supermarket. There was a great response, and the children spent many hours sorting, stacking, arranging, rearranging, categorizing, and pricing the packages. The containers were arranged on shelves that had been improvised from hollow blocks placed along the walls of each of the refrigerator boxes. The packages were priced 1, 2, or 3.

Since everything had to be stored away each Friday, the classifying and arranging began anew each Monday. Therefore, all of the children had many opportunities to participate in all aspects of the entire experience. They learned that the pictures on the labels of the packages could help them decide where an item belonged. Cheese, eggs, and milk belong in the dairy department. Ice cream could be kept in either the dairy department or with the frozen foods. Soap powder should not be stored next to the dry cereal, even though the boxes containing the two products are similar in size, shape, and color.

Retaining the idea of the supermarket, but varying the activity, the teacher drew horizontal lines on some poster board to represent shelves. She asked the children to look through magazines and cut out pictures of various grocery items to paste on the shelves. But they were not interested in this kind of categorizing and finally said they would rather work with the actual containers. The project was abandoned.

The children, however, were intensely interested in the next activity, which was making fruits and vegetables. A paper slightly heavier than tagboard was provided along with rich mixtures of red, green, yellow, orange, and deep purple fingerpaint. Each child painted one piece of paper with one of the colors. He then drew his own original fruit and vegetable shapes on his painting with a black marking pen. The shapes were cut out, and we then had a fascinating assortment of imaginative, odd-shaped, but fresh-looking produce. The various items were neatly arranged in slots cut into a large piece of poster board.

For several weeks each morning's activities centered around the store. The cash register was expertly operated by one child after another. This was an extremely popular activity, so cashiers were changed frequently during shopping hours. The shoppers spent a great deal of time getting dressed for their excursions. Gloves, hats, purses, and other items all came from the dress-up supply. The children experimented with many different types of items to use for pretend money. Sometimes real pennies were provided. Eventually, the food boxes had been sorted, stacked, bought, and sold so many times, that they began to need mending and patching. Some had been handled, inspected, opened, and closed so often that they were beginning to lose their shape.

We decided it was time to have a close-out sale. The boxes were transferred to the art supply table. Each child was allowed to select three favorite boxes to paint. Dark brown and dark blue paint with a little white added seemed to cover the printing on the packages better than other colors. Light colors of paint did not work well at all. Some of the packages had waxy or foil coatings so the teacher added a little detergent to the paint to make it adhere better. She could also have used wheat paste. The small size of most of the packages challenged the child's muscular control as he tried to apply the paint neatly with the relatively large brush. The child faced a demanding problem-solving situation as he struggled to figure out how to paint all sides of his box without smearing the sides he had already painted. He was delighted to discover that his old worn boxes looked fresh and new after they were painted.

A few days later the children arrived to find the classroom set up for a new activity—Box Sculpturing. On one table they found all their freshly painted supermarket containers lined up in a row according to size. On another table several bottles of white glue and rubber cement, Scotch tape, masking tape, scissors, string, and yarn had been set out in a large aluminum foil baking pan. The children were told they could choose any of the containers and fasten them together however they wanted to. Many of the projects took several days. No one seemed to have any trouble mastering the mechanics involved. If a child was unable to glue one piece to another he taped it. If taping didn't work, he would try to hold it while the glue set. Each new variation on his box sculpture introduced a new problem to solve. The child gained valuable experience in determining spatial and size relationships and discovering how physical objects fit together.

As a final box project before school closed for the summer,

the older children decided to construct a city. The teacher supplied some new cardboard boxes of many sizes and shapes along with a tempera-detergent paint mixture, white glue, masking tape, and other fastening materials. The teacher recognized each child's growing desire to produce representational objects and knew that with his experience in box sculpture and painting she could let him proceed freely with his own plan. The result was a delightful collection of houses, buildings, and cars. To complete the project, the children painted a large background mural to hang behind their city. At first glance the mural seemed to be totally abstract, but a careful examination revealed an imaginative painting of trees, flowers, sky, and ground.

These experiences, from the first beginning play with floor blocks through to the building of a cardboard city, were all part of the creative developmental art experience. They were *creative,* because the ideas originated with the child. Each experience served to motivate a succeeding experience. Once the flow of creative thought was started, imaginations became active, inventive actions took place. The activities were *developmental* because they changed in response to the developing needs and abilities of the child. They gave him the opportunity to carry, haul, stack, pack, unpack, classify, catagorize. Each child participated in group planning activities, and his ease and self-confidence in social relationships were correspondingly increased. He progressed from using materials symbolically to creating representational and recognizable shapes, forms, and objects. Finally, these activities were *art* experiences, because the teacher maintained an environment in which each child was allowed maximum creative freedom. As the child applied skills and ideas that he had acquired through home and school experiences, the teacher served as a facilitator, rather than a critic, thus further adding to his self-esteem and his ability to be artistically productive.

The Art Party

On the morning of the art party there was an acute sense of anticipation in the air. The two teachers with their two assistants felt it. Their thirty-two four- and five-year-old students felt it. Perhaps it began when their director had suddenly asked them to rearrange their schedules so that the entire group could go out to the playground together at 9:15, shortly after they had arrived. It was a brisk day. The sun was shining, but the air was

The Art Party.

cold. The movement on the playground was vigorous as the children climbed on, jumped over, and crawled under the equipment. Every wheel toy was in use. The rocking boat had a continuous stream of passengers coming and going. The tree-house platform was resounding with laughter.

When the children returned to their classrooms at 10:15, everything had been made ready. The folding wall between the two adjoining rooms had been pushed back. One half of the room was cleared of tables and chairs. Here the children sat down on the floor to have their mid-morning snack of juice and crackers.

In the other half of the room, all the tables were crowded together. At each table a different type of art activity had been set up. The children would find clay, collage materials, Styrofoam, easels, paint, chalk, crayons, scissors, paste, and a variety of paper.

Through careful planning, a feeling of space had been created—yet the closeness of the tables was deliberate. Here children could work at their own projects in their own places and yet be closely enough involved with others nearby that the electricity of creative accomplishment and emotional satisfaction would flow from one to another.

One teacher put some lively classical music on the record player, a few balloons were let loose among the children, and they were invited to go across the room and find a place to work.

The orderliness with which the materials had been set out, the casualness of supplementary materials, the placement of the tables and chairs, and the planned predominance of different colors in different areas of the room all made it comfortable and easy for each child to find something to do. Everyone became deeply involved in his own activity. From time to time the children would

change places. For the most part, the adults found that they were
in the way, and they gradually drifted to the other side of the
room to become onlookers. Their number gradually increased,
for everyone who passed the open doors of the rooms was drawn
into the group by the intensity of feelings that prevailed.

It was a magical hour, one that was strangely contradictory.
There was a dramatic tension, but at the same time there was
a feeling of relaxation. It was noisy and busy, but also still and
quiet. Here was creativity.

The following day, the workshop was repeated. The three-
and-a-half-year-olds were invited to join the group. To accommodate them, rolls of paper were put down on the floor, together
with crayons and chalk. Because of the younger age of some of
the children, the working time at any one activity was somewhat
shorter. But the same feelings of creative accomplishment prevailed as the children worked side by side. Age differences went
unnoticed. Usually restless, aggressive, or hyperactive children
were deeply occupied. Throughout the room there was a feeling
of complete and mutual involvement.

When the materials were used up and the time for lunch grew
near, the record player was turned off and the children were
drawn by the rhythmic beat of a tambourine to the cleared area
of the room. There they jumped and rolled and bounced. They
flew like birds and grew like flowers, then sang enthusiastically
in perfect unison:

> Are you laughing, are you laughing, laughing with me?
> Laughing with me?
> We are all now laughing. We are all now laughing.
> Happily. Happily.

Gradually, the spell was broken. The children returned to their
own classrooms with their own teachers. Tables were put back
in place and the folding door was closed. Each person who had
been involved, child and adult alike, had extended the dimensions
of his own existence.

The Art Dance

Another type of special art event is the Art Dance. Though similar
to the Art Party in that a very large group can participate at
one time, the motivations and the goals are entirely different.
In the Art Party, we have a variety and abundance of materials,

working areas close together, many children doing the same thing, a constantly changing musical background, limited physical space in which to move, and great earnestness displayed by all.

The Art Dance is characterized by a limited suply of materials restricted in variety, large sizes of paper, spacious working areas, freedom to be close together or far apart, freedom to change activities at any time, a constant repetition of the same musical accompaniment, and a general atmosphere of gaiety and abandon.

The Art Party increases the child's ability to concentrate, and expands his creative awareness in a general atmosphere of creative industry. The Art Dance, on the other hand, is primarily geared to increase the child's auditory-motor and visual perception and to produce a general overall growth in sensory awareness as body, mind, music, and media all flow together.

The Art Dance came about one day in early spring when doing something special seemed to be in order. Enthusiastically I suggested that the teachers and children all go outdoors to look for the early signs of spring. While they were gone, I cleared the classroom of all furniture except for two small tables pushed against one long wall. Murals the students had painted the day before were put up along the wall behind the tables. Here and there cardboard cutouts of children dancing and jumping set the stage for the coming gaiety.

On the tables I placed a few small cans of tempera paint and brushes, a few assorted crayons, some oil pastels and colored chalks, and several percussion instruments from the rhythm band set. I scattered in a haphazard pattern on the floor large pieces of paper, some rectangular and some circular. Two long rolls of paper 12″ wide were also put down. Finally, in the center of the room, I set out some collage materials and glue bottles on two pieces of dark construction paper.

When the children returned with their teachers, the record player was playing softly "Round and Round the Village." The children displayed little surprise in seeing the changes that had taken place, since they were accustomed to changes. As they recognized the promise of new experiences, their eyes sparkled brightly and they asked, "What are we going to do?"

I invited them to sit down on the floor and discuss it with me. We talked a little about spring, and about how it makes you feel inside when you see all the growing things getting ready to say, "Hello. I'm here." Some of the children's comments were, "It makes me feel I like you," and "I want to sing happy," and, "I think I want to scream!" I replied, "I'll tell you what I would

The Art Dance.

like you to do. You can use any of the things you see around the room. Listen to the music, make up an art dance and while you're dancing, I'll look into your faces and then I'll know how you feel. You may use the paints, the crayons, the chalks, the glue, or the musical instruments. You may use any of the pieces of paper, but you must share everything and take turns. Paint, or color, or glue, or dance, or sing. You may do all of these things whenever you feel like doing them and you may do them any way you like to do them."

The children were quickly on their feet, ready to make their own discoveries. To explore. To experience. To respond.

The children were *not* told, "Do whatever you want to do." This only leads to confusion and uncertainty. The success of this experiment was at least partially due to the clearly defined limits which had been set. The children were given a choice of materials to use within the framework of a carefully structured environment. But they were told only that they could paint, color, glue, sing, or dance. They were given instructions but they were still *free* to do those things when they felt like doing them and in the way they wanted to do them. On their own initiative the children one by one took off their shoes and began to dance around the room.

The only adult assistance required was starting the non-automatic record player over and over again. Near the end of the activity an adult directed the cleanup which was also done to the same music as part of the whole experience.

For 45 minutes each child expressed his mood, released his tensions, and worked out his feelings through art and music. Everywhere movement and rhythm were accompanied by experimentation and involvement. The various types of activities constantly interacted. The children responded particularly deeply because they had all participated for at least several months in creative developmental art activities. Each child had been constantly challenged to make maximum use of his body and his mind as an integrated whole. When the Art Dance was suggested, each child was able to accept the opportunity naturally and to participate with the full enjoyment of one who had been helped to see beyond the surface of his environment.

Discovery Corner

The Discovery Corner is a special area of the classroom that contains materials that the child does not ordinarily use or that he has been allowed to use only occasionally. The area can be just large enough for only one child at a time or it can be an entire table set up so that several children can work at once.

Individual sets of materials can be prepared for the child to take from a supply center to an area where he may want to work. Or the child may select the items he wishes to use and make up his own individual set. It can be set up by the teacher, or it can be part of the day-to-day, free-play activities.

The materials can be put in trays, lazy Susans, divided boxes, or similar containers. Just be sure that the materials are offered in a neat, colorful, and attractive way. Include such items as:

Stapler	Kleenex	Paper clips	Metallic paper
Scissors	Pipe cleaners	Plastic triangle	String
Ruler	Oil pastels	Pinking shears	Colored pencils
Paper fasteners	Charcoal	Yarn or thread	Watercolor pan
Paste	Ballpoint pen	Glue	and brushes
Carbon paper	Paper punch	Cellophane	Paper

Add any other materials you wish. The greater the use of *your* imagination in equipping and setting up the Discovery Corner, the greater will be the child's use of his imagination in discovering for himself what to do with the materials provided.

The Imagination Box is an attractively decorated box or other container that you have prepared for use by one or two children at a time. It is similar to the Discovery Corner in that it is a means of enlarging the child's experiences in self-discovery and experimentation. You may have several such boxes, each one individually prepared. In the box you place selected collections of surprises with which the child can create his own happening. He is not told to "make something" with the materials, but he usually will. However, he may prefer simply to investigate, arrange, and play with the items. This, too, is an enriching experience. An Imagination Box might include:

- Feathers, Styrofoam squares, pipe cleaners, strips of construction paper, two pieces of felt, some ribbon.
- Several pieces of metallic paper from a wallpaper book, small box of sequins, jar of glitter, felt scraps, paper punch, white glue, yarn.
- Graph paper, an almost empty bottle of red India ink with a good watercolor brush, gummed paper scraps, a piece of cardboard, masking tape, cellophane tape, scissors.

Your collections can be fantastic. Let your ideas run free. Just be sure that whatever you put in the box will stick or color or mark or fasten. For example, if the box contained only wax paper and watercolors, the child could not invent anything. He would only discover that watercolor won't adhere to wax paper.

If the materials are presented with care and in an attractive manner, the children will handle them with care. Children learn by example. To develop in the child the ability to direct his own behavior, remember that he will pattern that behavior after the behavior and attitudes of others in his environment, both at school and away from school. His creative attitudes are directly dependent on your creative attitude.

Displaying the Child's Art Work

Displaying the child's art work lets him know that you really like it and that you consider his creative efforts to be of value. Matting or framing his art work will make the display more attractive. However, don't allow the lack of time to prepare mats prevent you from putting the child's work up where it can be seen. Simple mats and frames can be easily made from paper.

To make a mat, use a piece of construction paper, fadeless art paper, or any other paper that is larger than the picture that is to be mounted. Select a color that harmonizes with one of the colors in the picture, or use black or white, both of which are always effective and will harmonize with almost any picture. Mount the picture on the mat by simply attaching it with pins, two-sided tape, transparent tape, or rubber cement. (Rubber cement will not cause the paper to shrink, but most other kinds of paste and glue will.)

Display the matted or framed pictures in groups mounted on corrugated display cardboard, poster board, illustration board, or on the bulletin board. The pictures in each group should have some degree of uniformity in the types of mats or frames used and in the way they are displayed. They should be arranged in a way that will provide a general overall pattern of harmony.

Pictures can be grouped according to the ages of the children who made them in order to show the developmental progress of child art, or they can be grouped according to kinds of projects in order to show the variety of activities in which the child has participated. The best way to handle multi-colored displays is to group the pictures according to their dominant color.

Holiday Activities

In the pre-school setting, holidays should be observed as simply as possible. Young children are often overexposed to holiday observances. The excitement can lead to emotional overstimulation and sometimes to physical exhaustion.

Most teachers, including me, have used traditional holiday motifs and symbols over and over again. There is a need in our lives for tradition and comfort in the use of familiar symbols. Too great an emphasis on traditional forms, however, may discourage creativity. It is possible to enrich the child's life by encouraging creative experiences in holiday art.

Any of the ideas that have been discussed in this book may be used in holiday art projects. Through the use of appropriate colors, special papers, and other materials, your everyday art projects can take on a seasonal air. They will reflect the spirit of the traditional motifs, whether or not recognizable symbols are used. You will find additional suggestions in the sections on Paper Shapes Through the Year in Chapter 2 and in Color Guide Through the Year in Chapter 3.

Listed below are some suggestions to help you make a collection of materials to use for collage and construction and for other art projects. From this list you may want to select items to help teach certain concepts. Of course, you do not have to keep all of these items on hand. These suggestions, however, should help you accumulate an interesting and varied collection of your own.

Acetate, colored
Acorns
Acorn tops
Allspice
Almonds
Aluminum foil
Apple seeds
Apricot seeds

Ball bearings
Balsa wood
Bamboo
Bark
Basket reeds
Beads
Beans
Belts
Bias tape
Blotter paper
Bobby pins
Bolts and nuts
Bones
Bottle caps
Bottles
Boxes
Brads
Braiding
Broken parts
Broken toys
Buckles
Buckram
Burlap scraps

Cancelled stamps
Candles

Candy wrappers
Cardboard scraps
Carpet samples
Carpet warp
Cellophane scraps
Cellophane tape
Chains
Chalk
Checkers
Cigar bands
Cigarette wrappers
Clock parts
Clothespins
Cloth scraps
Cloves
Coffee filters
Coffee grounds
Coins
Combs, broken
Confetti
Construction paper
    scraps
Contact paper
Cord
Corks
Corn husks
Corn kernels
Costume jewelry
Cotton batting
Cotton puffs
Crepe paper scraps
Crystals

Dice
Dominoes

Drapery samples
Dried beans and
    peas
Dried flowers and
    grasses
Dried seeds
Driftwood
Dry cereals

Easter grass
Egg cartons
Eggshells
Elastic
Emery boards
Embroidery thread
Erasers
Evergreens
Eyelets
Excelsior

Fabrics
Faucet washers
Feathers
Felt scraps
Film spools
Filters
Fish tank gravel
Fishing lures,
    hooks removed
Flashbulbs, used
Flint paper
Flocking
Florist's foil, foam,
    tape

Flowers, artificial
Flowers, dried
Foam packing of
  many shapes
Fur samples

Gauze
Gift wrap paper
Gimp nails
Glass beads
Glass mosaic rocks
  and pieces
Glitter
Gold thread
Gold jewelry parts
Grains
Gravel
Gummed labels
Gummed notebook
  paper reinforcers
Gummed paper

Hair netting
Hairpins
Hair rollers
Hardware scraps
Hat trimmings
Hooks

Ice cream sticks
Inner tube scraps

Jewelry pieces
Jewelry wire
Junk of all kinds
Jute

Key rings
Key tabs
Keys

Lace
Laminated items
Leather scraps

Leaves
Lentils
Lids
Linoleum scraps

Macaroni
Mailing tubes
Map pins
Marbles
Masonite
Meat trays, paper
Meat trays,
  Styrofoam
Meat trays, trans-
  parent plastic
Metal scraps
Metal shavings
Mirrors
Mosquito netting
Moss, dried

Nails
Newspapers
Noodles, dry
Noodles, wet
Nut cups
Nuts

Oilcloth scraps
Orange seeds
Orange sticks
Origami paper
Ornaments

Paint chips
Paper baking cups
Paper clips
Paper dots from
  computer paper
Paper fasteners
Paper products of
  all kinds
Paper tubes
Pebbles

Pill bottles
Pillboxes
Pinecones
Pine needles
Ping-Pong balls
Pins of all kinds
Pipe cleaners
Pits
Plastic bottles
Plastic foam
Plastic scraps
Popcorn
Potatoes
Pumpkin seeds

Q-tips
Quartz crystals
Quills

Raffia
Recording Tape
Rhinestones
Ribbons
Rice
Rickrack
Rock salt
Rocks
Rope pieces
Rubber bands
Rubber tubing

Safety pins
Salt crystals
Sandpaper
Sawdust
Scouring pads
Screening,
  plastic or wire
Screws
Seals, gummed
Seam binding
Seashells
Seedpods
Seeds

Sequins
Sewing tape
Shoe laces
Shot
Silk scraps
Skewers, wooden
Soap
Soldering wire
Spaghetti
Sponges
Spools
Spray can lids
Stamps, savings
Stars, gummed
Steel wool
Sticks
Stones
Straws, broom
Straws, drinking
String
Styrofoam

Tape, cellophane
Tape, masking
Tape, mystic
Tape, plastic
Tape, Scotch
Tape, sewing
Telephone wire
Thistles
Threads
Tiles
Tinkertoy parts
Tissue paper
    scraps
Tongue depressors
Toothbrushes
Toothpicks
Torn paper scraps
Twigs
Twine
Typewriter ribbon
    spools

Velvet scraps
Velveteen
Vermiculite

Wallpaper
Warp
Washers
Wax candles
Weeds
Wood scraps
Wood shavings
Wooden beads
Wooden dowels
Wooden wheels
Wool
Wrapping papers

X-ray plates

Yarns

Zippers

INDEX

Entries printed in *italic* type refer to illustrations. Entries printed in SMALL CAPITAL Letters refer to activities and projects. References to the learning and development that result from the creative art program are listed as subentries under Conceptual Understandings and Results.

183